Leading with New Eyes

Incredibly well written and very enlightening. Great examples and stories. Full of wisdom ... Take some time from your increasingly complex day to explore!

Dr Brian O. Underhill, Co-author of *Executive Coaching for Results* and Founder and CEO of CoachSource

B H Tan raises a crucial question: Why great companies fail? These companies look inward and become complacent. Leaders need to look with new eyes and become explorers. The book gives the keys for that transformation. Great reading!

Juan Antonio Fernandez, Professor of Management, China Europe International Business School (CEIBS)

Beautifully written and jargon-free. The author's discussions of self-awareness and leadership creativity are admirably clear and insightful. Highly recommended to all existing and aspiring leaders.

Mitch McCrimmon, PhD, Self Renewal Group

The first leadership book that shares the Asian perspective in such an interesting and engaging manner. The real-life cases will resonate deeply with all of us. Highly recommended to new and senior leaders alike, East or West. Time to pause and take up that mirror.

Susan Ho, Senior Regional Mars University Manager–Asia

The use of stories as living lessons imparts a personal touch ... Very much like having a personal coach. The provocative questions embedded in these pages make you pause and think deeply about leadership and creativity.

Professor Philip Choo, CEO, Tan Tock Seng Hospital, Singapore

Should be on the desk of everyone working in the private, public and not-for-profit sectors. For those who want to be more than just a custodian, who want to explore, grow and transform themselves and their organizations. For those who want to coach executives powerfully. Indeed for anyone who wants to lead self and others. I can't wait to use this book with my leader-coachees.

Su-Chzeng Ong, Executive Coach and former senior leader in an investment bank

Drawing on a wide range of ideas from the complexity sciences to ancient Eastern philosophy, this book will stimulate you to think about how you can lead your team to collaborate, be creative, solve complex challenges and seize opportunities for your organization to flourish. Encouraging you first to explore your strengths and understand where you have opportunity to grow, the book then provides you with ideas and examples of how you can develop into an explorer leader — one who can lead creatively through challenging times.

Louise Kovacs, CEO, Madston Black Singapore

B H Tan brings his extensive experience of working with leaders from East and West to create a thought-provoking assessment of the challenges facing modern organizations. Only by reinventing themselves can they create a virtuous spiral of sustainable growth.

Andrew Stanleick, VP and General Manager, Coach Inc, Malaysia and Singapore

This book takes us on a profound journey to decode the DNA of creative leadership. It is a treasure trove of ideas on creativity from different eras, disciplines and cultures. In this age of complexity, only leaders who seek a larger purpose will have the stamina and flair to keep reinventing their organizations.

Margit Oswald, Partner, osb Wien Consulting GmbH

This splendid book raises hard questions about the prevailing Western-centric view of organizations as mechanistic and rational. It's a strong advocacy for organizations to be seen as living systems. I particularly like the discussions about meditation and mindfulness. Getting in touch with our inner self may be the most effective way to cope with complexity. A must-read for leaders in the East and West.

Georg Remmers, VP Human Resource Development, Heraeus

A pragmatic view of creative leadership with lots of metaphors, anecdotes and stories that readers will relate to. Leadership is as much an art as it is a science. We must lead with both the head and the heart.

Yun Seong Yong, General Manager, Microsoft, Asia-Pacific Operations Center

Finally a leadership book that bridges the best of Western thinking and Eastern wisdom. We can't continue to rely exclusively on analytics and big data in decision-making and leading. B H Tan makes a compelling argument for leaders to tap into their inner wisdom as well. First know thyself. Then act mindfully. I wish his call for connectedness and authenticity will resonate globally.

Antje Boijens, Founder, Boijens kultur und management

A book full of wisdom ... Great insights and food for thought for leaders who are exposed to a multicultural environment.

Younes Alaoui, CEO, Pirelli Egypt

This is indeed an eye-opening book. Leaders who want to be more creative must habitually get on the balcony to spot trends and see larger patterns.

Helen Liu, HR Director for APAC, Murex

A unique guide on creative leadership, powerfully illustrated through fables, stories and cases from both Eastern and Western cultures. The penetrating questions the author raises are provocative. They encourage readers to reflect on and explore new leadership perspectives. Recommended for all leaders, emerging and experienced.

Spencer Liao, Director of Human Resources, TSMC, Taiwan

The key to success in a global marketplace is the ability to master multiculturalism. At L'Oreal, we are mindful about creating the right values and a climate of engagement for people in all countries we operate in. Through his wisdom and questioning approach, the author challenges leaders to think and reflect. Let's not expect standard answers in today's volatile environment. It is up to us to discover what is right.

Shalin Chuang, Manager, Learning for Development Asia-Pacific, L'Oreal

Leading with New Eyes

*How Explorer Leaders Unleash Creativity
in Their Organizations*

B H Tan

LEADING WITH NEW EYES: HOW EXPLORER LEADERS
UNLEASH CREATIVITY IN THEIR ORGANIZATIONS

Cover design and image by Prakasit Palakawong Na Ayudhya.

10 9 8 7 6 5 4 3 2
CTP COS
20 16 15 14

When ordering this title, use **ISBN 978-981-4575-20-1** or
MHID 981-4575-20-8

Printed in Singapore

CONTENTS

Part Four: Leading Wisely

ACKNOWLEDGEMENTS

In the mid-1970s, upon graduating as an engineer, I harboured dreams of carving out a career in the world of machines, systems and technology. All it took were three years working in a chemical plant for me to reach the proverbial fork in the road. The cut-and-dried world of data, facts and analytics could not sustain my interest. I had come to the conclusion that it was the human side of business that would be my passion.

What you hold in your hand is a compendium of the rumination and lessons learnt working with leaders in the East and West. In my early years, I had thought that the best business leaders were Cartesians. These are logical thinkers who can reduce any difficult problem into manageable components and — through sheer power of reasoning and analysis — find certainties in any situation. In the 21st century, the environment is much more complex and volatile. Leadership is about making judgement calls about the unknown and, indeed, the unknowable. While we must first start by examining the Cartesian possibilities, ultimately we must call upon our head, heart and guts. This is where the left and right hemispheres of the brain converge.

I am grateful and indebted to many teachers, colleagues, clients and friends who have helped shape my thinking and made this book possible. First and foremost, hats off to the sages and great masters of a bygone age on whose giant shoulders I have stood. They include Heraclitus, Descartes, Pascal, Confucius, Buddha, Lao Zi, Zhuang Zi, Plato and Marcus Aurelius.

There are numerous contemporary authors and teachers — past and present — whose works have informed my writing. Chief among them are Peter Drucker, Warren Bennis, Bill George, Daniel Goleman, Joseph Badaracco, Zenger and Folkman, R.L. Stevenson, Carl Jung, Richard Wilhem, Philip Zimbardo, Viktor Frankl, Ram Charan, Ronald Heifetz, Rooke and Torbert, Fritjof Capra, Margaret Wheatley, Leo Tolstoy, Philip Tetlock, Isaiah Berlin, Charles Lindblom, Carol Dweak, John Kotter, Howard Gardner, Herbert Benson, John Ratey, Jon Kabat-Zinn, W. Somerset Maugham and Sir Arthur Conan Doyle. Appropriate citations to these sources — as well as those not mentioned here — have been made in the respective pages of the book as well as in the Endnotes.

This book has gained immeasurably from the insights, encouragement and counsel of many friends, colleagues and clients who took time from their busy schedule to read the early drafts, either completely or partially: Marshall Goldsmith, Su-Chzeng Ong, Mitch McCrimmon, Leslie Chong, Louise Kovacs, Younes Alaoui, Margit Oswald, Georg Remmers, Spencer Liao and his colleagues at TSMC, Antje Boijens, Woon Peng Ziady, Philip Choo, Chew Kwee Tiang, Vanu Gopala Menon, Pek Sze Min, Tan Li San, Khor Check Kim, Helen Liu, Shalin Chuang, Johannes G. Hesse, Wendy Tan, Liak Teng Lit, Audrey Lee, Susan Ho, Shereen Kaur and Sarah McArthur.

To the following people who have written kind and generous endorsements, I shall be eternally grateful: Marshall Goldsmith, Juan Antonio Fernandez, Brian Underhill, Mitch McCrimmon, Younes Alaoui, Su-Chzeng Ong, Andrew Stanleick, Philip Choo, Louise Kovacs, Margit Oswald, Antje Boijens, Yun Seong Yong, Helen Liu, Georg Remmers, Susan Ho, Shalin Chuang and Spencer Liao.

And finally, kudos to the wonderful team at McGraw Hill led by Senior Acquisitions Editor Gerald Bok. This book is far better for their astute and professional guidance.

Whatever redeeming qualities you find in this book are due to the inestimable contributions of all the people mentioned above. Any shortcomings and omissions that remain are my own.

The real voyage of discovery consists not in seeking new landscapes but in having new eyes.

Marcel Proust (1871–1922)
French novelist

INTRODUCTION

... to travel hopefully is a better thing than to arrive,
and the true success is to labour.

Robert Louis Stevenson (1850–1894)
Scottish novelist, poet and essayist

I first chanced upon this thought from Robert Louis Stevenson, a 19th century Scottish novelist, poet and essayist when I was growing up in Singapore in the early 1970s. At that time, I didn't fully comprehend what he meant. But his words piqued my curiosity and, strangely enough, they have remained in my mind ever since. After graduating in engineering, that bastion of left-brain thinking, I was quickly caught up in the rat race, striving to climb the corporate ladder in a number of US multinationals. Everything I did revolved around working with teams of people to meet business

objectives and financial targets. To say that I was focused on the journey rather than the destination in that phase of my life would be disingenuous. All too soon, 20 years had whisked by.

Then I embarked on my second career as a leadership consultant; this was about 15 years ago. In this capacity, I work with leaders in the private and public sectors in Asia, the US and Europe. These are the high-potential executives slated for pivotal positions in their organizations. They range in ages from the 20s to the mid-50s, across different nationalities. Managers, directors, vice presidents, presidents, inhabitants of the C-suite and CEOs — these people stand out from their contemporaries. They are the *crème de la crème*: persons of high intellect, are ambitious, fast moving and high achieving. I am engaged by their companies to facilitate their development as leaders in preparation for greater responsibilities that are to come.

A Glimpse into Leaders' DNA

Working with these leaders has provided me deeper insights into their DNA. A typical leadership development engagement lasts 12 months and is done one-on-one. In many cases, there are also workshops involving the leaders and their senior leadership teams.

In the course of our interactions, I am both privy, and privileged, to hear their innermost thoughts and learning: ideas, opinions, decisions, prejudices, doubts, struggles, angst, actions, the highs and lows and their reflections. Over time, a fascinating and intriguing pattern starts to emerge, which addresses the following questions:

- Who are you?
- What is your level of self-awareness?
- What drives you to behave the way you do?
- How in touch are you with your core values?

- How do you define success?
- How do you make sense of the world around you?
- How do you make judgement calls in ambiguous and complex situations?
- How do you engage, influence and inspire?
- Do you ever behave out of character? What can you learn about this?
- As your role becomes more complex, how do you stay ahead of the curve?
- How can you lead more creatively?
- Have you ever felt in over your head? What should you do then?
- How does one become wiser with age?
- How do you renew yourself continually for the long haul?
- How do you tap into a higher realm of understanding in turbulent times?

Thirty-five years and 250 leaders later, spanning the East and West, as I sieve through what I have learnt, a singular lesson emerges.

Organizations rise and fall in a cyclical pattern of transformation and change. Upon reaching the crest of success, decline is already underway. This results from inward orientation and lack of diversity. Though the downturn is painful, not all is lost. Creative minorities[1] may appear on the scene. If they succeed in upending the status quo, they will reinvent their organizations. However, if powerful adherents of the old way refuse to budge, disintegration becomes inevitable.

This book is about a simple idea. Leaders will reinvent their organizations only if they *Lead with New Eyes*.

Explorers and Custodians

There are two kinds of leaders. Some relish challenges and assignments that stretch them. They do not fear not knowing, and see difficulties and setbacks as opportunities for personal growth. Indeed, they seem to be marching to a different drumbeat from the rest of the organization: always curious and asking questions, exploring and seeking new and even iconoclastic worldviews. Being great listeners and questioners, they connect well with people within and without their organizations. They have the ability to hold in constructive tension short- and long-term business needs, make sense of ambiguous and complex situations and function effectively in paradoxical situations. They lead in a way that is consistent with their own core values. Because they are self-assured, assertive and influential, they may unsettle colleagues, including bosses. There are times they push the envelope so much that they may cause some chaos and destabilization. That is the price they feel their organizations must be willing to pay to continually renew and reinvent themselves. Such people remind us of *explorers*, always looking into the wide yonder in search of new frontiers to conquer.

And then there is an overwhelming majority of leaders who bring a much needed sense of stability by steering a steady course. These leaders form the backbone of the organization. They provide clear directions and purpose to others, and ensure that systems, processes and resources are in place for the short to medium term. They are operationally very competent, will develop their people and invest in building collaborative relationships with peers and other stakeholders. They will inspire co-workers to keep stretching themselves. Their dedication is unquestionable. They consciously scan the environment and will adapt and adjust. In crises and times of peril, they will pull out all stops, including initiating painful changes, to bring the organization back to even keel. Such people are the *custodians*, those who protect, raise operational efficiency and expand the home base.

In innovative organizations that continue to renew themselves again and again, we need both explorers and custodians. They are Siamese twins, inseparable, interdependent and provide a powerfully complementary relationship that will enable organizations to navigate between opposing forces: uncertainty versus certainty, instability versus equilibrium, change versus status quo and the future versus the present. Leveraging each other's unique capabilities and perspectives, they set off a virtuous spiral of growth that rejuvenates and sustains.

The Rise and Fall of Great Organizations

In most organizations, the custodians will far outnumber the explorers. That is because human beings generally prefer control and predictability. As organizations grow, the corporate culture which favours the explorer mindset at the beginning will slowly but surely become more conservative. With continued success, a sense of complacency and even arrogance will pervade such organizations. Would-be explorers soon become co-opted into the systems and will think and act as custodians.

What is the prognosis for such organizations in the fast-changing, increasingly complex and unpredictable environment of the 21st century? Acclaimed business thinker and author Jim Collins[2] has spent a great deal of time studying the rise and fall of some of the greatest companies in history. In his view,

> *Every institution is vulnerable, no matter how great. There is no law of nature that the most powerful will inevitably remain at the top. Anyone can fall, and most eventually will.*

A similar observation can be made about powerful cultures and countries in history.[3] They rise and fall as well. Examples are the Roman, Ottoman, Ming and Mughal empires. In recent times, Britain and Japan rose to superpower status and then declined.

What factors lead to the fall of powerful companies? When enterprises become great, their leaders will start to see success as an entitlement because they have found a surefire recipe that will guarantee their success. They turn inwards and stop seeking deep insights and ideas that will set them apart from the competition. Believing that they are indomitable and too big to fail, complacency quickly sets in. They become bureaucratic, fat and inflexible. When they face setbacks, they try to explain them away and succumb to denial. The once nimble and entrepreneurial outfit is now an aging and lumbering elephant that can't navigate the swirling currents around it. Precipitous decline follows soon after.

Here are some recent examples of once-mighty corporations that have fallen: Polaroid, Kodak, Nokia, Motorola, Toshiba and BlackBerry. And now only a year or so post-Steve Jobs, Apple appears stodgy compared to Samsung. When will its glorious reign as the world's most valuable company end?

From Managers/Leaders to Custodians/Explorers

Readers may recall that in the last few decades of the 20th century, there was much debate about the differences between management and leadership. Leadership scholars Abraham Zaleznik[4] and Warren

Bennis[5] delineated the contrast quite starkly. Bennis sees leaders as those who master the context and managers as those who surrender to it. He goes on to explain a list of other differences which are enormous and crucial.

Most people recognize that management and leadership can't be separated. Indeed, they are linked and complementary. Managers who keep their heads down and keep plugging away will soon be blindsided. And leaders who keep thinking about the future without taking care of current realities will lose their mandate quickly.

The 21st century has upped the *ante*. Organizations must be reinvented again and again. The manager–leader dynamics must now be replaced by the constructive tension between the custodian–explorer (See Appendix 1).

Creativity Is the Most Important Leadership Quality

DO THIS?

In the IBM 2010 Global CEO Study[6] based on face-to-face interviews with 1,500 CEOs spanning 60 countries and covering 33 industries, four key points were highlighted:

- Most of the CEOs said that they are operating in a substantially more volatile, uncertain and complex environment and they expect complexity to increase in the years ahead.
- More than half of the CEOs worry about their ability to manage the increasing complexity.
- Western CEOs expect the centre of economic gravity to shift to the developing markets and foresee increasing stricter regulations ahead.
- Creativity is cited as the most important leadership quality.

In this context creativity is more about creative leadership, rather than having a creative leader at the top. It is about having a climate of creativity in which long-held and cherished practices are open for scrutiny and, if found irrelevant, are replaced by new, even disruptive, ideas and means of execution. It also means having creative leaders who go on to identify and nurture other creative leaders. Such leaders are willing to make deep business changes to realize their strategies. They must be comfortable with, and welcome, disruptive innovations.

Collaboration Is the Number-One Trait CEOs Seek in Employees

In the latest IBM 2012 CEO Study[7] involving 1,700 CEOs in 64 countries, the theme of complexity continues to be highlighted. It is about increasingly interconnected organizations, markets, societies and governments. CEOs recognize that to succeed in this new world of rapid change, they need to create more open and collaborative cultures, and encourage employees to connect and learn from each other. Seventy-five per cent of the CEOs interviewed cite collaboration in their people as critical. The report suggested three imperatives for outperformance:

- Empowering employees through values.
- Engaging customers as individuals.
- Amplifying innovations with partnerships.

This will require a more distributed and collaborative management style that engages with a new generation of workers, partners and customers. It emphasizes:

(And even when the organization is performing well, CEOs must occasionally break from the status quo and introduce external catalysts, unexpected partners and some intentionally disruptive thinking.)

Metaphors About Organizations

In the last 100 years the predominant imagery of an organization[8] is that of a machine with discrete and multiple parts. Responsibilities are organized into separate functions. Organization charts define how the machine works: the number of pieces, how they fit with each other and which pieces are the most important. Perhaps, that is how the expression *mere cogs in the corporate machinery* came about.

In the 1990s, the business world was abuzz with a new concept called *reengineering*. This revealed the deeply entrenched belief that organizations are indeed machines. Reengineering soon became the world's leading management fad. For many companies which were facing bloated bureaucracies, deeply-rooted inefficiencies, intense foreign competition and other ills, it was *the* solution. However, those which jumped on the reengineering bandwagon soon found themselves in an ugly situation. In their haste to reduce cost, they invariably went down the path of restructuring, layoffs and too-often failed change programmes. In an article in business magazine *Fast Company*, Thomas H. Davenport,[9] one of reengineering's creators, wrote:

> *The rock that reengineering has foundered on is simple: people. Reengineering treated the people inside companies as if they were just so many bits and bytes, interchangeable parts to be reengineered. But no one wants to be reengineered.*

Physicist turned organizational theorist William Bygrave believes that the machine metaphor of organizations has been very much influenced by the engineering background of many organization thinkers, including Max Weber, Frederick Taylor, Alfred Chandler and Michael Porter. Due to their training they see organizations as rational and structured environments. Perhaps it is not all that surprising given that the concept of organization arose during the Industrial Age.

In the last few decades a more useful and appropriate metaphor has emerged. This was catalyzed by Arie de Geus in his book *The Living Company*.[10] In and by itself, the idea that organizations are a human community hardly seems like a revolutionary thought. However, the truth is, even today, the machine image still holds sway in companies. For instance, the president of a company recently posed this question to me: "What is the return on investment for this leadership development programme for my people?" It was as if he was asking me to quantify the expected increase in output if he upgraded the equipment in his factory.

When companies invest in developing their leaders, the expected increase in output is not immediately quantifiable. However, many months, and dare I say, years later, such leaders will slowly but surely transform the climate in their organization. As the culture evolves such intangibles as a greater sense of purpose, optimism, collaboration, commitment and creativity become manifest. And now will come the harvest: increased productivity, sales, outputs, profitability, etc.

Given the realities of globalization, 24/7 digital communication, unpredictable, unstable, non-linear and fast-paced interconnections between nations, firms and people, and profound changes across technology, market and society, the living system metaphor is becoming more relevant and helpful. It provides us an eminently useful guide to thinking about complexity — the defining feature of the business environment in the 21st century.

Convergence of Eastern and Western Thinking

In the study of management, it is the thinkers in the West who have played the leading role in the last 100 years. But, despite a rich tradition of scientific discoveries and cultural ascendency in many civilizations in Asia, the East has contributed little to the lexicon of management thinking. Are there now signs that the wisdom of Eastern thinking is slowly gaining recognition among Western management theorists? That is what I am seeing, so I am hopeful that this trend will continue. Why my optimism? I see signs of convergence in two key areas:[11]

- A shift from the more mechanistic and fragmented Western view to a more organic and holistic Eastern view of the world. It may be described as an ecological worldview where all individuals, events and actions are not separate, but interrelated and connected. We are embedded in and dependent on the cyclical processes of nature.
- There is also a growing awareness that rational knowledge which measures, quantifies, classifies and analyzes may

not be sufficient in the age of increasing complexity. Though this way of thinking has served mankind admirably for hundreds of years, thinkers both in the East and West now believe that we need to tap into a higher realm of understanding in order to ensure a more sustainable future.

In the East since time immemorial, the focus has always been to see the whole, with interconnecting networks within, rather than to focus on the individual parts. There is an ancient Sufi saying that captures the essence of this philosophy brilliantly:

> *You think because you understand "one" you must also understand "two", because one and one make two.*
> *But you must also understand "and".*

Ancient Daoist philosophy[12] that can be traced all the way back to 500 BC is about the art of living harmoniously with nature. Daoists see all things in the universe as constantly changing in orderly cycles. Thus, the steady-state in the machine metaphor is unsustainable. Nature, and hence businesses, is a self-organizing system in perpetual interaction of *yin* and *yang* forces or energies. What is stable will gradually become unstable, and then through renewal, will become stable again. It is a natural order of things for ebbs and flows to occur like the waves lapping the shore.

In the last few decades, ground-breaking studies in sociology, positive psychology, neuroscience, anthropology, the humanities and behavioural economics in the West have shed more light on how humans behave. Far from being the rational utility-maximizing individuals, man is not primarily the product of conscious, linear thinking.[13]

We know that our brain consists of two half-brains: the left and right hemispheres. The left hemisphere excels in conscious, linear and logical thinking and the right hemisphere interprets the world through pictures, emotions and intuition. For us to lead a creative, meaningful and successful life, we need to have both sides working in concert. That is when we can access the *unconscious* parts of our mind where the most impressive acts of creativity reside.

In his book, *Strangers to Ourselves*, Timothy D. Wilson[14] of the University of Virginia writes that the human mind can take in 11 million pieces of information at any given moment. But according to the most generous estimate, we are only conscious of 40 of these. Wilson adds:

> Some researchers have gone so far as to suggest that the unconscious mind does virtually all the work and that the conscious mind may be an illusion.

This discovery runs parallel to what sages and mystics in the East have always known: that our ordinary waking state of consciousness is severely limiting. Because of our frenzied pace of life, we fall into a robot-like way of seeing and doing and thinking. During such moments we lose touch with ourselves and the rest of the world. This is a dream-like state that the Buddhists call *ignorance*, or even mindlessness.

Through the practice of meditation, mindfulness is achieved. This enables us to live our lives more fully with access to the full spectrum of our conscious and unconscious possibilities. In this way, channels to deep reservoirs of creativity, choices and wisdom in us are opened. Both meditation and mindfulness are in fact universal and timeless concepts. They are known and practised by

the great religious traditions of the world such as Hinduism, Daoism, Buddhism, Christianity and Islam. Socrates (469–399 BC) and Marcus Aurelius (AD 121–180) knew about the benefits of calmness through meditation. William James, the father of modern psychology, taught that the habit of voluntarily bringing back a wandering attention would be the root of judgement, character and will.

How to Derive the Maximum Benefits from This Book?

If you are a CEO, one of the senior leaders or a member of a team, how can you become a member of the *creative minorities*? What additional repertoire of skills and tools will you need? How will you engage your people to collaborate and discover possibilities amid the fog of complexity, uncertainty and unpredictability?

This book aims to help. It will enable you to become a more sagacious explorer as you navigate through the new landscape. The framework that will guide this truly transformational journey consists of four dimensions:

- Raising self-awareness
- Serving a larger purpose
- Seeing new possibilities
- Leading wisely

Each dimension will be the focus of one of four parts of this book. There are altogether 15 short chapters, each addressing a topic that is central to creative leadership. The ideas and practical suggestions that you will be exposed to will draw upon thoughts and wisdom from the East and West, interwoven into a powerful strand. There will also be real-life cases that will exemplify concepts being discussed.

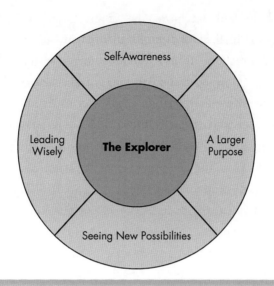

Before you start reading the chapters, do turn to Appendix 1. It is a diagnostic assessment to determine where you are in the continuum between custodian and explorer. Next, I recommend that you pause and ask yourself the following questions:

- Where is my organization heading?
- Who is responsible for reinventing my organization?
- If not me, then who? If not now, when?

Learning to lead creatively is not an armchair activity. The leader's voyage of development is not an easy one. Some people change little in their lifetimes; others change substantially. While genetics has an undeniable impact, human nature is not fixed. We can all learn to become better leaders. But only if we become more self-aware and work at developing ourselves over the long haul.

As you go through each chapter, pause and reflect frequently. Have a journal beside you. Jot down your thoughts and questions.

If you wish to find out more, the Endnotes section will provide suggestions for further reading. At the end of each chapter, under the heading Practices, I have raised a few questions for you to consider. Don't just reflect. Identify a couple of actions to take. Start by transforming yourself.

Finally, there are three appendixes. Appendix 1 is the diagnostic assessment mentioned earlier. In Appendix 2, I have chosen to tell the stories of two healthcare practitioners who are transforming the complex arena of healthcare services in Singapore and India. Finally, I have consolidated in Appendix 3 a list of questions found at the end of all 15 chapters. This serves as a handy guide for reflection and action. Also, it is a quick overview of the entire book.

And now, it is time to circle back to Robert Louis Stevenson's quote featured at the beginning of this section. The classic novel *Siddhartha*[15] by Hermann Hesse — German novelist, poet and Nobel Prize winner in literature in 1946 — is a story of the spiritual journey of self-discovery of a man called Siddhartha during the time of Buddha (563–483 BC).

At the end of his quest, Siddhartha ran into an old friend, Govinda, who was also a spiritual pilgrim. They had pursued different paths to seek *nirvana*. While Siddhartha had attained enlightenment, Govinda had not. To Govinda's query, Siddhartha said:

> *Seeking means: to have a goal; but finding means: to be free, to be receptive, to have no goal. You, O worthy one, are perhaps indeed a seeker, for in striving towards your goal, you do not see many things that are under your nose.*

When we pretend that we already know *the path* to take right at the outset, we rush headlong with a great sense of focus and urgency. Soon we find ourselves in an ever-narrowing ravine and become stuck. Having no preconceived notion of the final outcome, and open to new ideas and cues as we venture into the uncharted waters of the 21st century, we become explorers. What infinite possibilities await us!

Leading with New Eyes

PART ONE
WHO ARE YOU?

*One day Alice came to a fork in the road and
saw a Cheshire cat in a tree.
Which road do I take? She asked.
Where do you want to go? was his response.
I don't know, Alice answered.
Then, said the cat, it doesn't matter.*

Lewis Carroll (1832–1898)
Alice in Wonderland

Chapter 1

KNOWING
YOURSELF

Be yourself; everyone else is already taken.

Oscar Wilde (1854–1900)
Irish writer and poet

The first thing that I do with leaders who participate in my leadership development programmes is help them raise their self-awareness. They are asked to complete a self-reflection worksheet in which they respond to questions as candidly as they can about themselves, their behavioural styles, their strengths and their weaknesses and their values. Then I conduct a series of confidential interviews with people who know them well. In many instances, I may suggest that they complete some personality assessments such as MBTI (Myers–Briggs Type

Indicator), the Hogan Assessment System or the DISC. DISC is the acronym for Dominance, Influence, Steadiness and Compliance. It is a behavioural assessment tool.

From the feedback through the interviews and data in the assessment reports, the leaders will have a good sense of the similarities and differences between their self-image and the way others view them. Generally, there will be surprises, both positive and negative.

Knowing the Real You

Every leader has both strengths and shortcomings. This is so all the way down from the CEO to the first-line manager. To Confucius (551–479 BC), the first and most important responsibility of any leader is to discover and cultivate his inherent qualities. He asks:

> *If you cannot improve yourself, how can you hope to succeed in improving others?*

Warren Bennis,[1] renowned pioneer in contemporary leadership studies, writes:

> *"Know yourself," was the inscription over the Oracle at Delphi. And it is still the most difficult task any of us faces. But until you truly know your strengths and weaknesses, know what you want to do and why you want to do it, you cannot succeed in any but the most superficial sense of the word.*

Some years ago, the 75 members of the Stanford Graduate School of Business Advisory Council[2] were asked to recommend the most important capability for leaders to develop. Their answer was nearly unanimous: self-awareness. What is self-awareness? Is it sufficient to know one's strengths and weaknesses and play to one's strengths while circumventing one's weaknesses? Let's consider the lessons learnt by a talented manager whom I shall call Indra.

INDRA was a brand manager of a leading French consumer products company. She had recently relocated from Mumbai to Manila as a participant of her company's international development programme (IDP). In India she was identified as a high-potential leader. In her five years there, starting as an intern fresh from the famed India Institute of Technology, she had already chalked up a sterling record of successes. And the new posting was a chance for her to gain international exposure and be stretched further.

An integral part of the IDP was leadership coaching for the participants. I was her executive coach. Three months into her posting in Manila, Indra and I had our first meeting. She came across as soft-spoken and gentle while exuding youthful enthusiasm, curiosity and intensity of purpose.

In her self-reflection report, she described herself as fast moving and keen to develop her staff. She also said that as she was younger than all her subordinates, she feared she lacked *gravitas*. When I interviewed peers and staff, they all mentioned how much they respected her for her vision, professionalism and can-do attitude. Indeed, many saw her as a role model. However, colleagues, especially direct reports, pointed out that as she had a naturally commanding presence, she was intimidating. During business reviews, if the discussions strayed

a little, she would look displeased and rap on the table with her right index finger.

That Indra was well-respected by colleagues in Manila came as no surprise. However, she misjudged that her relative youth would be an impediment in her new environment. Unconsciously, she overcompensated for her insecurity by displaying a take-charge style a little too frequently.

The Philippines was a new country for her. People there are generally friendly, easygoing and gregarious. They are respectful towards their bosses. However, if they are uncomfortable with their bosses, there will be distance and mistrust.

Indra was calm and receptive when the feedback report was discussed with her. She realized quickly it was a blind spot for her: she had not taken time to pause and see herself through the eyes of her new colleagues. In the months ahead, by becoming more conscious of her body language and softening her demeanour, she was able to steer meetings in the right direction while inviting others to participate openly. But a few months later, Indra hit another speed bump.

Although her relationships with colleagues improved somewhat, it became clear that Indra's business results were falling short of projections. And she was leading the company's most prestigious brand, no less. Indra was concerned and rightfully distressed. She said that she was doing everything to engage her people and to invite their ideas and suggestions. She sensed though that the gusto and esprit de corps that had ignited her team in Mumbai was nowhere evident here. What was holding everybody back?

At her request, I spoke again to her team members and her peers. This time Indra was deeply shocked when I shared my findings with her. Despite her attempt to soften her style, people said they didn't trust her. She didn't seem authentic. Signals she sent were extremely conflicting. Although she was always calm and measured, non-verbal cues revealed impatience and aggressiveness. She hardly spent time socializing after work. Colleagues were convinced that all she wanted to do was to excel in her assignment here and then secure a promotion for her next posting.

Badly shaken, Indra nonetheless admitted that she had always been an overachiever all her life. "Why do I drive myself like crazy?" she asked rhetorically. We had a long conversation that day. She reflected on her childhood, growing up in a poor family. Her parents slogged incessantly to put her and her three siblings through school. Being the oldest child, she naturally became the family's torchbearer. Even as she spoke, her father's voice resonated constantly in her mind: "You will do our family proud by becoming the first woman country manager of your company in India!" Indra realized that she was living not the life she desired, but the life that her parents had dreamt for her.

Authenticity

Why didn't people trust Indra? For that matter, how do we decide whether to trust someone? The most straightforward answer is that when we sense a disconnection between a person's words and actions, we become wary. Over time wariness turns into mistrust as we observe more signs of inconsistency. First impressions are hard to change. Once formed, people will selectively look for evidence to justify their suspicions. Bill George,[3] former chairman and CEO of Medtronic and now professor at Harvard Business School, has spent many years studying leaders and their traits. He believes that leadership begins and ends with authenticity — that is, being the person you are meant to be.

Leaders who are authentic genuinely desire to serve others through their leadership. Helping others to become better is a greater impetus than securing power, money or prestige for themselves. They are as guided by qualities of the heart as they are by qualities of the mind. George is convinced that although many people have natural leadership qualities, it takes a lifetime of personal development to fully become outstanding leaders.

In summary, to be an authentic leader, we first need to know ourselves and be ourselves. Authenticity is further underpinned by five essential qualities:

- Having a sense of purpose
- Possessing a moral compass defined by values and character
- Leading with the heart
- Establishing enduring relationships
- Demonstrating consistency in words and actions

Leadership is a deeply personal quality that we exude. We can't succeed unless we have a sense of who we are and are willing to show that to people around us. It is not about exhibiting a bunch of traits that we pick up from a book or by imitating someone we think is a great leader.

After getting over the shock that people didn't trust her and that it was all about her, Indra decided that she had to reinvent herself as a leader. Deep down, she recognized that she was by nature very competitive and driven. Even if her parents had not planted the idea into her head about moving up, she would still have aspired for it. She wasn't ashamed of this. This was the fire in her belly. Yet, it wasn't about climbing up by stepping over others. It was more to challenge herself to go as far as she could.

Looking back at her days in school and in Mumbai, she knew that people actually mattered a lot to her. She enjoyed the camaraderie with her colleagues and found her relationships with them mutually rewarding. She had always enjoyed their brainstorming sessions during which boundless creative ideas seemed to pop up with ease. She didn't see success as a personal badge of honour. It was a means to an end. With greater success, she could better impact and influence her environment to be more *human-centric*, as she put it. That also allowed her to open more doors for her colleagues.

Why did she then behave out of character? It was initially the sense of disorientation in a new country and culture. This was followed by the fear of not getting accepted as she was the new kid on the block. This led her to distance herself. Without the bonhomie that she was used to, she became more and more disconnected.

Indra impressed me with her resilience. The experience was a wake-up call and she quickly bounced back. She initiated one-on-one sessions with all her subordinates and other colleagues in the weeks ahead. She acknowledged that she was sending conflicting signals and shared her lessons learnt. Her colleagues were very supportive and congenial. Her openness and sincerity won them over. In the months ahead, she showed her true self consistently and fearlessly: a uniquely paradoxical ability to balance relationships with the drive for results.

Indra went on to serve three years as brand manager with great success. Not only did the business grow significantly year over year, her team was recognized as the most productive and creative. When she left to become general manager in Singapore, one of her team members succeeded her. One more was promoted to head a new brand in another country as a candidate of the IDP.

Having a sense of purpose

Why are you in a leadership position? Is it for the power, prestige and financial rewards? Is it because it is natural to climb higher, given your talents and education? Is there a larger purpose that has yet to be discovered?

Without a real sense of purpose, we will be adrift in the corporate environment. Power, prestige and financial rewards are like trophies that we pick up. Lacking a real purpose, they become proxies. One CEO said to me blithely: "My pay package is a scorecard. Though I have gone way past the need to work for money, it still defines how successful I am. My pay is public knowledge as my company is listed."

Most leaders have a high need for achievement. And how they progress in their career provides the most tangible evidence that they are moving forward. Thus, they focus on achieving that sales target for this quarter, shipping this new product, getting approval for this proposal, securing that promotion, getting tenure at the university, and so on.

All these lead to immediate gratification. In contrast, they might have noticed that people around them aren't collaborating but working in silos. Or that employee turnover is increasing. Or that people are working unusually long hours and may be in danger of burning out. And even that their own home life is unfulfilling and filled with tension. Yet all these seem like noise in the environment. Why be distracted by them? Onward with the real business at hand!

If we look back at how companies start off good and then gradually drift into mediocrity and even disasters, we find an unmistakable pattern: there is this very human tendency to focus on endeavours that offer quick gratification. A wise friend calls it *going for the cheap thrills.*

There are, however, a small minority of people who are able to be more detached, and see career and life through a larger lens. They intuitively know what matters most and will allocate their time and resources appropriately. To them, leadership is a privilege to serve others. When you genuinely serve others, you unleash a virtuous cycle of energy in the organization. The spirit is lifted. We become inspired by the larger cause that we are pursuing.

Possessing a moral compass defined by values and character

Our values are those aspects of our life that we consider of central importance to our existence. They are our key drivers and form part of our identity. We are happiest when we are working in an environment, or participating in activities, that are consistent with our values. Conversely, people find it stressful to have to act contrary to their values.

Examples of values are integrity, fairness, security, recognition, fun, etc. Values are like our moral compass. When we are buffeted by frequent changes and forces that are beyond our control, we need a true north that we can take reference from. Otherwise, we will be whipsawed around.

Talk is cheap as they say. In our long leadership journey, we will be tested again and again. When we lose our bearing, we stop becoming effective. Soon our colleagues will become disillusioned and disenfranchised. These will be our *defining moments.*

Leading with the heart

In the Introduction, we discussed two metaphors for organizations. The dominant metaphor for the last 100 years is a machine. This harks back to the Industrial Age. Though we are now in the 21st century, the machine metaphor still casts a long shadow at the workplace. In many parts of the world, working in companies is like working in a sweat shop.

Foxconn is the world's largest contract manufacturer with more than a million workers. It supplies products for the likes of Apple, Sony, Hewlett-Packard and others. A couple of years ago, it achieved notoriety when there was a spate of suicides by their workers in China in protest against the ghastly conditions in their factories and dormitories.

Rugeley[4] used to be a mining town in England. In the 1990s, the mines closed and most people lost their jobs. In the summer of 2011, there was cheer when Amazon set up an order fulfilment centre for its operations. Hundreds of jobs have been created, which is a godsend for people who had been unemployed for a long time. Inside the massive warehouse, workers are required to push trolleys guided by handheld computers on where to walk to and what to pick up when they get there. Each person walks between 11 and 24 km each day. Boosting productivity the *kaizen* way (i.e. achieving success through small continuous improvements), employees are constantly measured and watched. What do the people of Rugeley make of this? While they are grateful for the employment, some people said: "It is like being in a slave camp."

In the 21st century the biggest challenge is complexity and unpredictability. The organizations which are operated like machines will not survive. Companies must start to behave like a living community. When the hearts and minds fuse, ideas and creativity will flourish. This is the lifeline that companies need. And these are inherent qualities that are waiting to be harnessed, *for free!*

Establishing enduring relationships

When employees walk into the workplace every day, they possess a power of discretion that no manager can take away. Consciously or unconsciously, they will ask themselves: "How much should I contribute?" How they decide depends on their relationships with their leaders. If they feel respected and trusted, and are willing to entrust their hopes and future in their supervisors, they will go the extra mile. Otherwise, they will contribute to the statistics on disengaged people that appear in employee engagement surveys around the world.

Leaders need to create a climate that inspires their people to give of their best. Inspiration does not come as a result of a series of steps or pronouncements that come from up above. To inspire is to infuse someone with emotions. This means engaging through the head, heart and guts. As most leaders have made their mark by displaying their intelligence, domain expertise and finesse in delivery of results, this is a territory that they either avoid or tread with trepidation.

Psychologist Daniel Goleman[5] first popularized the concept of emotional intelligence (EQ) in 1995. There is a compelling message for all of us. In organizations, you will hardly ever find someone

failing because of inadequate intelligence. It is lack of EQ that makes or breaks them. EQ will determine how effective we are in establishing an enduring relationship with others. There are two main aspects in EQ:

1. *Self-awareness:* How well we know ourselves and how we regulate our emotions in order to impact others constructively.

2. *Others-awareness:* Understanding others' emotions and inspiring and influencing others positively.

Demonstrating consistency in words and actions

Starting off on the right footing is the first step. In the long journey ahead, many unexpected events await the leader. These are tests by which followers will be evaluating their leaders.

Leadership is about making *choices* and making decisions under pressure. What choices do we make? What behaviour is exhibited? Do we turn moody and nasty? When short-term results are falling short, what do we say to head office? How do we treat our people?

Someone said to me that it is easy to encourage people to take risks and be creative. The acid test will soon come. When crises erupt, what is our stand? In the face of moral ambiguities, confusion, deep conflicts, how do we react? What if a promising idea subsequently fails? What if someone makes a poor judgement call that results in losses to the company? Will we be there for them?

In this chapter, we have touched on many important qualities of leadership. The other chapters in Parts 1 and 2 will elaborate on them in greater depth. Chapter 2 will discuss that all-important

CHAPTER 1

Part One

quality called character that influences our choices in our moments of truth.

PRACTICES

Q1: What drives you internally? Name your top five values and rank them.

Q2: How will the people closest to you describe you, warts and all? Any surprises with reference to Q1?

Q3: What support do you need from the people closest to you to live your top values?

Q1   1 Justice
      4 Honesty,
      3 Integrity.
      5 Collaboration
      2 Customer Service

Q2   Dunno

Q3   Not much

CHARACTER
ABOVE ALL

---

*The content of your character is your choice. Day by day,
what you do is who you become. Your integrity is your
destiny — it is the light that guides your way.*

Heraclitus (535–475 BC)
pre–Socratic Greek philosopher

Once, I asked a group of participants towards the end of a weeklong leadership retreat to anticipate the single biggest question they would ask themselves at age 80 when they sat down to reflect on the story of their lives. They became unusually quiet.

These participants were in the prime of their lives, mid-30s to early 50s. All were the best and the brightest from their companies. Throughout the week, they had all been highly animated, even vociferous, weighing in on topics that ranged from company vision, to strategy, corporate social responsibility and leadership.

That morning it seemed that I was with a different group. Words did not come that freely, and some prompting was needed. After what was a long silence, they offered the following responses:

- Have I made the most of my life?
- What am I proudest about?
- If only I had ... !
- What have I done to help others?

There were quite a few quiet nods among the participants. Then, as though we had uncorked a bottle of champagne, they started engaging each other in a more emotive manner than I had noticed in the past few days. We had struck a chord lying deep inside each person. And now they had begun to partake in an *unnatural* discussion.

It is rare for movers and shakers to be contemplative. Far be it for them to gaze decades into the future and look backwards. For these action-oriented people, it is always climbing one mountain after another: new markets to penetrate, policy papers to write, deals to cut, ideas to sell. That day they put the nuts and bolts of real business on hold to debate the philosophy of life. They reached two conclusions:

- Life will be defined by a series of decisions made in response to situations.
- Most people don't reflect deeply about the judgement calls they make. Once a decision is made, they move on. It is the tyranny of time.

Here are two real-life cases that managers may encounter in the course of their work.

Case 1

YANG worked for a leading US technology company. A few years ago, he relocated to Kuala Lumpur to head up the Southeast Asian business. This was a big career move for him. Yang was a dynamic leader who put people at the heart of everything he did. He had great dreams for the business and the people. In the first few months he spent much time reaching out to colleagues at all levels to learn more about the business and to solicit views and ideas.

The employees warmed up to Yang quickly and saw in him a leader whom they could trust and relate to. He was a far cry from the previous head who was aloof and autocratic. The latter did not leave any lasting impression as he returned to the United States within a year to take up another assignment.

Things went very well in the first two years. Then came the Lehman Brothers banking collapse. This threatened to shatter the global capitalist order on both sides of the Atlantic. The US market started to weaken and the Euro zone countries went into a tailspin. As the company was deep in the red for the second year running, Wall Street was turning hostile.

The Executive Committee at headquarters in New Jersey went into a crisis mode. Everybody was panicking and focused on saving his job. Soon, they mandated a series of changes and deep headcount reduction across the global operations. Although the Southeast Asian business was doing reasonably well, the bosses wanted Yang to lay off a sizeable part of his workforce. Yang became very anxious and tense. This was the first time he had to do this. He and his senior team hunkered down over many nights to discuss various options they could adopt, short of letting people go. Quite a few innovative and yet practical ideas surfaced.

Yang emailed his global head Don to arrange for a huddle. Don's response was curt. The video call would be that night at 9pm Malaysian time. Only Yang should be present. None of his team members were to attend. The video call was over within 15 minutes. Don was in a foul mood, like he was on the verge of a nervous breakdown. He was cold, peremptory and even dismissive. No, no, no, he kept saying forcefully. No other ideas, please! Just cut and slash. Also, be clear about protecting the company's intellectual property. Just round up the affected people, ask them to hand over their employee badges and have Security escort them out of the company's premises, pronto.

This wasn't the Don that Yang had known for the last few years! How one could change so dramatically under duress! Members of Yang's senior team were milling outside the conference room. He invited them in and told them what had transpired. He also mentioned Don's explicit instructions not to give any notice to affected employees. Yang and the senior leaders were perturbed by the turn that the company was taking. Respect for people had always been one of the company values. They all felt that Don's instruction would be in violation of faith with the employees. And of course, they conceded that Don had a point too: protection of the company's intellectual property.

The dreaded day arrived within a week. Throughout Southeast Asia, the respective site heads and their HR business partners met with each affected employee to explain the company's decision to reduce headcount. Each person was treated with dignity and compassion. Then, everybody was invited to the cafeterias at the respective sites. On a large LCD screen, Yang addressed the people in the various countries in a measured tone about the layoffs. Visibly emotional but still composed, he expressed his deep regrets to the people who were laid off and wished them well.

The following day, when Don learnt about what Yang had done, he was furious. But Yang kept his cool and remained unfazed. The storm blew over two months later. Yang and his business recovered. But Don, the global head, had lost all credibility with all his senior reports.

Case 2

JAMES, the marketing director, was in a dilemma. A year ago, he agreed to do a favour for an old friend. This person had a niece, Ellen, who was looking for a product manager position in James's company, the subsidiary of a large German multinational. James then made arrangement with HR for an interview. Apart from Ellen, there were other more qualified candidates. However, despite objections from his HR colleagues, James offered Ellen the job of franchise manager.

It didn't take long for him to find out that he had made a poor judgement call. Although Ellen had the experience and smarts, she had difficulty working with colleagues to launch new products and align on communications strategy. Many product launches were delayed. Clearly, Ellen was out of her depth: her franchise was floundering. As her immediate supervisor, James had to be personally involved on many occasions to prevent further mishaps. He also spent time coaching and guiding Ellen, but to no avail.

James called his old friend and let him in on the struggles that Ellen was going through. To his surprise, his friend said calmly that the same thing had happened in a previous position that she was in. Though she was clearly a bright person, having graduated top of her class in chemistry, she lacked empathy. Perhaps, James would be so kind as to arrange for a transfer to a role in research and development. James was miffed. Why hadn't his friend alerted him about Ellen's inability to work with people? His friend apologized profusely for not coming clean earlier.

Despite his own misgivings about Ellen, he went over to the director of research and development, a buddy of his. After much persuasion he succeeded in getting a transfer for Ellen. Six months later, he was chagrined to find out that Ellen had quit in a huff. She could not fit into the new environment.

Character[1]

Managers are constantly faced with a myriad of choices and decisions to be made throughout the day. They will respond in a variety of ways. Some will pause and weigh the pros and cons carefully. They slow down to seek clarity and composure. If necessary, they will ask for the counsel of friends, colleagues or family members. Yang was one such example. Though under duress, he kept a cool head and remained true to his values and principles. He was a mindful leader.

There will be many who are just too busy to pause and reflect. So caught up in the operational routine, they will decide on the fly with hardly a thought. It will just be another thing to get out of the way. Later they will rue their decisions. James was one such person. He led mindlessly.

Then we have leaders who get rattled easily. Many people in lofty positions up there fall into this category. In a crisis, they lose their cool and become callous and insensitive, concerned only with their skin. Don epitomized such a person.

For every individual, the decisions that are made cumulatively over many years will define his character. And character is destiny. The *Webster's New World College Dictionary* defines character as follows:

- A distinctive trait, quality or attribute
- The pattern of behaviour or personality found in an individual or group
- Moral strength, self-discipline, fortitude and so on

John Zenger and Joseph Folkman,[2] who conducted a groundbreaking study on the psychology of leadership, posit a leadership model as a large tent supported by five poles. Each pole represents a major element of leadership as follows:

- Character
- Personal capability

- Focus on results
- Interpersonal skills
- Leading organizational change

In this model, character is the centre pole with the other poles arranged at the periphery. In other words, character is the foundation stone. Without it, success is elusive and ephemeral. Long-term failure is certain despite all the talents and smarts that leaders may possess.

Yet, in my experience, corporations all over the world spend so little time looking into the character of leaders whom they wish to groom. Perhaps, it is because they think that there isn't much that can be done at this stage. Isn't character already formed and hardened like a crust by the time people become adults? Perhaps, it is because they don't know what can be done to mould somebody's character. And so they devote all their attention to the other four elements: personal capability, focus on results, interpersonal skills and leading organizational change.

Organizations will ultimately pay a price for this, a heavy price. In the course of their work, leaders will be tested in small and big ways. When tested, they will have to make decisions. How they decide will reveal their character. And in *defining moments*,[3] some leaders who are authentic will be guided by their moral compass. They possess the guts to do the right things and lift their organization up, even at great cost to themselves. Others reveal their feet of clay. Running scared, they bring others down with them.

Defining Moments

Joseph Badaracco, Jr. is the John Shad Professor of Business Ethics at Harvard Business School. For many years he taught an

MBA elective, *The Moral Leader*, which became very popular. Badaracco believes that character is formed through *defining moments*. A *defining moment* challenges us in an emotionally-wrenching way by asking us to choose between two or more ideals in which we deeply believe. Such challenges rarely have a single *correct* response.

Most of us know how to decide between a right versus a wrong. In a defining moment, the choice is not between a right and a wrong, but between a right and another right, or even a few other rights! The moral dilemma is much deeper as we have to choose between approaches which are right in some ways and yet not so right in other ways. How should we choose? Sitting on the fence is not an option. And time is of the essence. Such circumstances compel leaders to take a stand. Doing so reveals their values, principles and character. In such moments something that has been hidden or lying dormant is revealed. It surprises not only others, but themselves too.

Compared with Yang, James had a much easier challenge. It wasn't even a defining moment. The choice was between right versus wrong. Yet he failed the test, not once but twice. Yang's challenge was clearly a defining moment. Should he obey Don's instructions? Doing so would be right as it would not put the company's intellectual property at risk. Yet it was not right because that wouldn't be treating his people with the respect that they deserved. If he wanted to keep faith with his people, he would have to spend time explaining to them what the company had decided and attending to their emotional needs. Yet this would have put him on a collision course with Don. The company's intellectual property might be put at risk, and he and his senior team members would be vulnerable. Although caught between a rock and a hard place, Yang decided to lead with his head, heart and guts. The rest he left it to providence.

Making Choices Mindfully

To make wise choices, we need to accept a paradoxical principle: *slow down in order to speed up*. This means inculcating a habit of pausing and reflecting. This need not be a long-drawn process. It starts with an inner trigger that counsels us softly: "Here's a potential landmine. I must pause before deciding."

Leaders lead stressful existence. There are always judgement calls to be made. Learning from others, especially role models, by observing them as they deal with difficult situations will help. Being open-minded and exposing ourselves to diverse perspectives prevent us from being blindsided by our own prejudices. Sometimes when we observe other people's behaviours, we become judgemental and critical. "I will never do this" we tell ourselves self-righteously. Confucius suggests a more helpful approach:

> When we see men of a contrary character, we should turn inwards and examine ourselves.

Reading literary classics and the biographies of great men and women in different eras will be another source of enlightenment and self-cultivation. More generally we may refresh our mental landscape regularly by taking an interest in the arts. Why so? Because, as dean of theatre Madeline Puzo[4] at University of Southern California puts it,

CHAPTER 2

Part One

You should be afraid of art, it can change your life. You should be afraid of artists. By nature, they are subversive. They ask questions, challenge authority. They do not accept the status quo.

Are you making choices mindfully? You don't need to go far away to look for real-life challenges. They are present in your workplace right at this moment. Will there be instances when to everybody's surprise, no less yourself, you act out of character? Why and when will this happen? We examine this in Chapter 3.

PRACTICES

Q1: Can you think of a defining moment that you have encountered? What have you learnt about your character?

Q2: You are the boss. You have a high-flying sales director who is a star in the industry. She and her team outperform year over year, resulting in strong top- and bottom-line growth for the company. She is a *prima donna* though. She rides roughshod over everybody in the company. Sparks are flying and there is static in the atmosphere. You fear that she will quit if you speak to her about her toxic behaviour. How will you handle this?

THE **LIGHT** AND THE **SHADOW**

If my devils are to leave me,
I fear my angels will take flight as well.

Rainer Maria Rilke (1875–1926)
Austrian poet and novelist

There is a part of us human beings that is hidden inside that we would rather not know or talk about. It is a disowned aspect of us, if you will. The great Swiss psychiatrist Carl Jung called it the *shadow*.[1] This is the negative side of us, the unpleasant qualities that we prefer to hide. When Carl Jung formulated this idea, he believed that what is known consciously about ourselves is in the light. But that part of us which stands in the light — whether it be a trait or an idea — will cast a shadow. The shadow is what we don't know because it is hidden by darkness.

Why should we be talking about this, which at first blush, sounds rather bizarre and fantastic? Here is some anecdotal evidence that may pique our interest further.

Examples of the Light and the Shadow

Dr Jekyll and Mr Hyde

In 1886, Scottish author Robert Louis Stevenson[2] published a novella entitled *The Strange Case of Dr Jekyll and Mr Hyde*. This is a sensational work about what is now known as a mental disorder called split personality. The story revolves around a Dr Henry Jekyll, an erudite doctor, who struggles with the dual nature of his personality. Although he is kindly and respectable to his friends, he has a dark side which he expresses through an alter ego in the form of a mysterious and sinister Mr Hyde. Throughout the story, Dr Jekyll tries to overcome Mr Hyde. Eventually, the dark side wins and Dr Jekyll loses his life.

Powerful people who self-destruct

Robert I. Sutton[3] is a professor of management science at Stanford University. He has written extensively about powerful people who self-destruct when they were at the top. The causes are the two usual suspects: sex and/or corruption. And then there is extreme narcissism. The names of these fallen icons still ring in our minds: CIA director general David Pereaus, US president Bill Clinton, International Monetary Fund chief Dominique Strauss-Kahn, Hewlett-Packard CEO Mark Hurd, McKinsey & Co managing director Rajat Gupta, Taiwan president Chen Shui Bian, Philippines president Gloria Arroyo, and in China, powerful political star Bo Xilai.

Here in Singapore, despite our squeaky clean reputation, we have not been spared. Recently, there have been numerous high-profile cases of sex and corruption involving senior leaders in the government, its agencies, and even in schools and a university, no less.

Abraham Lincoln

The 5 November 2012 edition of *Time* magazine carried a fascinating story about Abraham Lincoln, the 16th president of the United States. It describes how historians were intrigued by Lincoln's use of the word *strange* to describe himself in his earliest attempts at writing his autobiography. Soon after his assassination in April 1865, newspaper editor Josiah Gilbert Holland[4] spoke with many people who had known Lincoln personally. He later published one of the first full-length biographies of the fallen leader.

Holland's wide-ranging conversations shed further light on Lincoln's use of the word *strange.* He found that nobody could agree on their measure of the man. Some said that he was extremely ambitious while others denied that he had any ambition at all. Similarly, people were equally polarized in their views about other aspects of Lincoln. Examples: the saddest *versus* the jolliest man that ever lived; a man of indomitable will *versus* a man without any will; and a tyrant *versus* a kind and brotherly man. In conclusion, Holland said Lincoln was the sum of his contradictions.

Why do very successful, accomplished and highly intelligent people self-immolate at the peak of their career? If their astounding ascent is guided by their light, it is their shadow that now precipitates their calamitous fall from grace.

Encounters at the workplace

Consider these incidents that you may come across in your daily life:

- One day, after braving the usual morning commute, you finally reach your office. No sooner have you sat down on your chair than you hear a knock on the door. Your eager beaver assistant wishes to have a few minutes with you rather urgently. You snarl: "Not now! Can't you see I'm busy?" As the hapless girl scurries out of the room, a voice goes off in your head: "What on earth got into me?"

- A high-ranking government official is known to be no-nonsense, and doesn't suffer fools gladly. He is a hands-on manager who will roll up his sleeves to ensure that the department is functioning at peak efficiency. Co-workers toe the line and will uphold a high standard of professionalism, except for one individual. This person consistently underperforms and misbehaves. Yet the boss turns a blind eye. He is unable to sit down and have a much needed difficult conversation with this individual.

- At the reception counter of a hotel, an irate guest is miffed because the hotel is overbooked. The information technology system is down and hence booking records are inaccessible. The person in front of the queue gives the front-office manager a hard time. You watch with a mixture of irritation and amusement. A thought bubble goes up in your head: "What kind of hotel is this? Serve her right!" Yet, when you reach the head of the queue, you are quite calm and forgiving. The visibly nervous lady behind the counter thanks you profusely for your kindness and arranges for you to be transferred to a nearby hotel.

Two Sides of the Same Coin

Lao Zi[5] was an older contemporary of Confucius. His name means *the Old Master* or more picturesquely, *the Old Boy*. Little is known about Lao Zi except that he could have been an archive-keeper during the Warring States period in ancient China. The classic manual on the art of living *Dao De Jing* or simply *The Dao*[6] is widely attributed to him.

The *Dao* was drawn from Lao Zi's close observations of nature. It reveals the wisdom of living systems, describing the patterns of energy within and around us. The Chinese call this vital energy *qi*, and the Japanese call it *ki*. *The Dao* consists of 81 poems written with grace and large-heartedness. They radiate a sense of humanity, humour and deep wisdom. It is the most translated book in history together with the Bible and the Quran.

Now in the 21st century, people from all over the world, including those in the West, continue to draw inspiration from *The Dao*. It has influenced such diverse fields as philosophy, psychology, politics and even the biological and physical sciences. Georg Wilhelm Friedrich Hegel lectured on *The Dao* at Heidelberg University in the early 1800s. Morihei Ueshiba, the founder of akido, based his non-violent martial arts on Daoist teachings. Carl Rogers practised *The Dao*'s philosophy in his therapy and work for peace.

In researching this book, I discovered that Carl Jung was a student of Chinese philosophy. For more than three decades he interested himself in the *I Ching*, the ancient Chinese *Book of Changes*. He also studied the works of Lao Zi and Confucius. In the foreword to the 1923 translation of the *I Ching* by noted sinologist Richard Wilhelm,[7] Jung wrote that such great minds as Confucius and Lao Zi should be carefully studied for the quality of thoughts they represented. He also recognized the *I Ching* as their main source of inspiration. He added:

> The ancient Chinese mind contemplates the cosmos in a way comparable to that of the modern physicist who cannot deny that his model of the world is a decidedly psychological structure.

The Dao is in fact a handbook for leaders, written to help them make wiser and more mindful choices by living in harmony with nature. With the increasing complexity that we are facing, it is even more relevant today. The notion of the coexistence of the light with the shadow is a theme that recurs throughout *The Dao*. It is also known as the complementarity of opposites or *yin* and *yang*.

Steven Pinker,[8] a Harvard College professor, has written about this age-old duality: the devil on one shoulder, whispering temptations, enticing us to act on sinister urges; and the angel on the other shoulder, holding us back with caution and consequences.

How do we apply these lessons in our work and life? For the rest of this chapter, I will discuss three areas:

- A strength overused becomes a weakness
- Creating a climate of engagement
- The danger of narcissism

A strength overused becomes a weakness

Leaders are frequently advised that to succeed, they need to know their strengths and weaknesses. Success will come only if they fully leverage their strengths. As for their weaknesses, don't get too hung up unless they represent potentially fatal flaws. Barring these, try to find a way to work around the weaknesses.

This is sound advice. But it is also true that we can take a strength too far. More is not always better and indeed when our strengths become overused, our shadow starts to reveal itself.

Consider the case of **JILL**, a highly-driven accounting manager with a streak of perfectionism. She possessed an admirable work ethic: every piece of work sent out from her department must be flawless. She was the first to office and last to leave. Everyone viewed her as the go-to manager. She was in fact enjoying the reputation that she had acquired. Besides, she had an immense capacity for hard work and details. To ensure everything was perfect, she personally reviewed the work of all her people. To her, she was just leading by example. To her people, many of whom were very experienced and competent, she was micromanaging because she didn't trust them.

Jill came to her senses only when three of her subordinates met up with her individually to suggest that she empower them more. It was either that or they would quit. Coincidentally, her boss had also expressed her concern that she was getting sucked into the weeds. Jill was expected to work more strategically. Jill was fortunate. She received a wake-up call before she could harm herself and others further.

Creating a climate of engagement

The desire to achieve is a major source of strength for individuals and the organizations they lead. It generates passion and energy which lead to sustainable high performance over the long term. According to a 35-year study by Hay Group's McCelland Center in Boston, businesses benefit when managers are achievement oriented. Productivity, revenue and innovation soar. But there is a dark side to the achievement motive.[9] By relentlessly focusing on tasks and goals, an executive or company can, over time damage performance. It demolishes trust, undermines morale and soon productivity and creativity take a big hit.

To create a strong climate that encourages trust, managers must recognize that the way they lead will be the determining factor. The McCelland Center study has identified six leadership styles that are generally practised, and their appropriateness depends on the situations and settings:

1. *Directive.* A command-and-control style that may become coercive. This is appropriate in a crisis or when managing someone who is underperforming or clueless. If used indiscriminately, it stifles creativity and initiative.

2. *Visionary.* Though it shows the way clearly, the leader gains employees' support by explaining the overall strategy and context. This makes goals clear, increases employee commitment and raises the energy level in the team.

3. *Affiliative.* The style emphasizes the person and his emotional needs over the job. Leaders who adopt this approach recognize that their people need greater emotional support and empathy because of personal or organizational distress.

4. *Participative.* This is a collaborative and democratic approach in decision making and getting things done. It is great in situations when people are competent and capable, and the leader may be new, have limited knowledge or formal authority such as in highly matrixed settings.

5. *Pacesetting.* Leaders drive by setting examples and personal heroics. They make clear the standards expected and follow up closely to make sure everybody conforms without exception. Such was the case of Jill. Over time, people will become disenfranchised. Such leaders will be swamped with work that their subordinates are more than equipped to do.

6. *Coaching.* Leaders take the time to develop people for the long term through building up their confidence and capabilities. Instead of telling them the answers, they encourage them to seek solutions on their own with the appropriate amount of guidance. This is an underused style that is powerful in bringing out the best in others.

There is no one best style of leadership. None is appropriate for all situations. The most effective leaders are able to use all six styles as required. In a study of 21 senior managers, it was found that managers who are able to create a strong climate of engagement exhibit the following:

- They employ at least four of the six styles of leadership.
- Though driven by the desire to achieve, they also have a need for affiliation and power.

The danger of narcissism

When leaders reach the peak, it is when we see their personalities writ large. Some start to act out of character. In extreme cases, they self-destruct. It was Lincoln who said,

If you want to test a man's character, give him power.

Talking about leaders, we usually start with the assumption that they are rational people. Yet, according to Manfred F.R. Kets de Vries[10] of INSEAD, irrationality is integral to human nature, and psychological conflict can contribute in significant ways to success. He calls this the *inner theatre*.

A key derailment factor in high places is narcissism. Narcissism is the profound self-centredness of many high achievers, which is both a constructive and destructive force. It can be extraordinarily useful and even necessary. It endows such leaders with a sense of supreme confidence in their ability and mission. How else can they divine the future and have the courage to push through massive transformation that society needs, and leave behind their legacy? On the world stage past and present heads of governments such as Singapore's Lee Kuan Yew, Malaysia's Mahathir Mohamad, the UK's Margaret Thatcher, Germany's Angela Merkel, and corporate leaders like Li Ka Shing of Hong Kong and Morris Chang of Taiwan, spring to mind.

On the flip side, narcissism can be destructive. When lacking self-knowledge and self-regulation, narcissists will start to believe their own rhetoric, and become enamoured with their larger-than-life image. When narcissism is mixed with hubris, the product becomes highly combustible. These are some of the indicators of dysfunctional narcissism:

- An overweening sense of self-importance.
- An oversized ego.
- A habit of taking advantage of others to further their own ends.
- An amazing sense of entitlement, that they deserve special treatment.

- A feeling that rules set for others do not apply to them.
- They are addicted to compliments and can never get enough.
- They are out of touch with reality and are unable to experience how others feel.

Working for a dysfunctional narcissist is a terrifying experience. Here is a real-life case that happened a few years ago in a European multinational that I shall call KDC.

RONNIE finally reached the coveted post of president, Asia-Pacific at KDC, a European engineering company. It had been 15 years doing what he called grunt work as a manager, director and vice president. He had always been outstanding in all he did. He knew that, and so did everyone else.

His biggest frustration for the longest time was with his bosses up there. Both the Europeans and the Asians. They were just too indecisive and cautious. But he had always kept his opinions to himself, confiding in nobody. Always showing supreme self-control, he was politically savvy and charming, and could finesse his way out of any situations. Most importantly, he always delivered on his commitments. Now at long last, he had cleared all hurdles and could steer the company to greater heights.

From day one, he was determined to signal that things would be different. He moved very fast, but always making sure that his bosses were behind him all the way. Within 18 months, he had reorganized his management teams throughout the

Asia-Pacific, doubled sales, opened up new manufacturing sites and distribution centres.

With his stellar success came a sense of entitlement and invincibility. He became arrogant towards his subordinates and even had shouting matches with senior colleagues at headquarters in Brussels. Based in Shanghai, he became a celebrity in business circles. He frequently hosted lavish golf events and dinners, inviting the rich, famous and powerful.

As his fame spread all over China, he started spending more time cultivating the press and less and less time minding the business. Almost as quickly as he had boosted the business, it started to decline. None of his lieutenants felt empowered to make major decisions while he was away on his frequent junkets with government officials.

Alarm bells were soon ringing in Brussels. When an audit was carried out by a team from the headquarters, they found a workforce completely demoralized and plagued by leadership and structural issues. Soon after, the CEO decided to part ways with Ronnie.

As we have said earlier, outstanding people all possess a certain amount of narcissism. If a person is a shrinking violet, the odds of going great guns are minuscule, to put it mildly. If so, why is it that some leaders are able to leverage the constructive side of their narcissism while sublimating their destructive impulses? This was an act that Ronnie couldn't quite pull off.

It is lonely at the top. People who have reached lofty positions frequently find themselves increasingly isolated. Unbiased and truthful opinions from people around them are hard to come by because *candour flees authority*. Wise leaders will work hard to create a climate where it is safe and comfortable for staff to express their opinions openly. This is easier said than done, especially in Asian cultures where people dare not offer differing views for fear of appearing defiant and disrespectful.

One highly effective way for bosses to understand how others are viewing them is through the 360-degree feedback system, in which opinions are sought from people at all levels anonymously. A prerequisite for genuine and candid feedback is a sense of trust for management. There must also be an assurance of anonymity.

Leaders who seek feedback must demonstrate fortitude and humility. There will be surprises, both pleasant and unpleasant. Be prepared to acknowledge the feedback and, more importantly, commit to making the necessary changes. Few leaders at the top have embarked on such a journey. It is not for the faint-hearted.

When Vineet Nayar[11] was appointed president of the Delhi-based information technology services provider, HCL Technologies, the company was losing market share and mindshare. He knew he had to transform its business model, starting with its corporate culture. Among a number of key actions that he pioneered was the *employee first culture*. HCL already had a 360-degree feedback system in place. However, it was not effective as employees weren't convinced that any good would come out of it. Nayar decided to lead by example by inviting employees to give feedback about him and posting the results on the intranet for all employees to see. He then identified the gaps in his leadership style and worked on what was important. Other managers soon followed suit. A few years later, in 2009, HCL had successfully transformed. It nearly tripled its annual revenue, doubled its market capitalization and was ranked by Aon Hewitt, a global talent, retirement and health solutions business, as India's best employer.

The higher leaders climb, the more likely they may slip and fall with grievous consequences for themselves and their organizations. To keep themselves grounded, they need to seek the views and ideas of people at various levels in the organization, especially the staff at the front line. These people are more likely to tell it the way they see it. In contrast, senior managers will tell bosses what is politically safe and correct.

In the days of the Roman Empire, when a conquering general entered Rome on his chariot, there would be a slave behind him whose job was to whisper,

You are human, Caesar; you are human.

The poem *A Fool's Prayer* by American poet Edward Sill contains many truths for the corporate chieftains of the 21st century. A court jester, who called himself a fool, touched the heart of a wise king when he pleaded for mercy and offered a moral lesson:

Not all who are great and mighty are wise.

The room became hushed. Deep in introspection, the king rose to depart from his guests. With much humility, he murmured:

Be merciful to me, a fool.

Embracing the Light and the Shadow

As *The Dao* advises, we possess both the *yin* and the *yang*. One cannot exist without the other. Much as we are uncomfortable

CHAPTER 3

Part One

with our shadow, we can't ignore it or try to drive it away like Dr Jekyll.

Nobel Prize-winning poet Derek Walcott's[12] four-stanza poem, *Love After Love*, talks movingly about greeting and accepting our whole self, including our disowned aspects and welcoming them back into our lives. In his masterful words,

> Give wine, give bread, give back your heart
> To the stranger who has loved all your life,
> Whom you abandoned for another, who knows you by heart.

PRACTICES

Q1: Have you ever overused your strengths? What is the impact on yourself and others?

Q2: When was the last time you observed someone behaving out of character? Perhaps, it might have happened to you? What can you learn about this?

Q3: In your long leadership journey, how do you ensure that you are able to embrace the light and the shadow? How should you apply Derek Walcott's advice?

Q4: Dr Philip Zimbardo,[13] professor emeritus of psychology at Stanford University, has done extensive research which shows that evil is something we are all capable of, depending on circumstances. He also asserts that we are just as capable of great heroism. What do you think? What

are the circumstances that will bring out the good or evil in us?

Q5: You are about to tap a well-regarded subordinate to a high office. You have seen his light thus far. Will his shadow manifest itself when he is up there?

PART TWO
THE MEANING OF YOUR WORK

*Work is difficulty and drama, a high-stakes game in which
our identity, our self-esteem and our ability to provide are
mixed inside us in volatile, sometimes explosive ways …
Work is where we can make ourselves; work is where we
can break ourselves.*

David Whyte (1955–present)
English poet

Chapter 4

SERVING A LARGER
PURPOSE

Ultimately, man should not ask what the meaning of his life is, but rather he must recognize that it is he who is asked. In a word, each man is questioned by life, and he can only answer to life by answering for his own life; to life he can only respond by being responsible.

Viktor E. Frankl (1905–1997)
Austrian psychiatrist and Holocaust survivor

When different people encounter the same situation, what will they experience? What do you see in the picture on the following page? Most people say it looks like a strange animal. Perhaps a hound or even a dinosaur. A small minority will pause for a while and then say, "Wait a minute! If we focus on the white space instead, it could be something else. Maybe they are the heads of three individuals in the midst of a conversation?" Another person may chime in: "Can even be three pots of plants!" And now something else happens.

Our vista widens and we start to see more possibilities than a minute ago.

How the Human Mind Perceives

According to the *Talmud*,

> We do not see things as they are.
> We see them as we are.

Neuroscientist Gregory Berns[1] explains that vision is not the same as perception. Vision is the process by which photons enter the eye and are transformed into neural signals in the brain.

Perception, on the other hand, is the much more complex process by which the brain interprets and converts these signals into mental images. And this is a rather individualistic process. In order to do the conversions, the brain takes plenty of shortcuts. To understand this, consider the bandwidth of the optic nerve — the main conduit of information from the eyes into the brain.

Its information flow has been measured, and it is estimated to be about the speed of a cable modem.

Many of us who use a cable modem to watch video over the Internet quickly realize there are compromises in terms of information flow: images tend to be pixelated and jerky. Similarly, even though our brains are being fed information at the same rate through our eyes, this is not how we see the world, because the brain is constantly filtering and making sense of what it sees. Thus, when we see something, we don't perceive it as an objective, but a subjective reality. How we make sense of events is based on our life experiences up to that point. There is also the impact of our attitude, character, personality, societal norms, work environment, and so on. Yet another set of contributing factors will be the prejudices, biases, thinking frameworks and assumptions. We may even lump all these into a bucket and call them common sense.

Human beings don't notice that they are breathing air. Similarly, fish swimming in the ocean aren't aware of the water around them. Common sense has the same effect on us. We don't see it anymore. It just defines us. And more importantly, it will determine how we choose to respond.

Let's consider a situation that is commonly encountered at the workplace. In organizations, people have different responsibilities and functions. Hence, their objectives will be different. However, in order to get their work done, people will have to collaborate. With different work objectives, priorities will be different. This frequently results in conflict. And there are two diametrically opposite ways to view conflict.

Most people are uncomfortable managing conflict. It is considered something that is negative. The usual approach is to escalate the matter to their bosses whom they expect to sort things

out. Then everything will be well defined and there will be no conflict. But as they will discover, involving the bosses may aggravate the disagreement further. Ill feelings may deepen. The conflicting parties will then try to minimize interaction with each other. This is the beginning of the silo mentality. When this disease deepens and becomes pervasive, it will tear the organization and people apart.

Another way to view conflict is that it is a force for good. When people come together, it is only natural that there will be dissonant views. And conflict is an opportunity to collaborate so that their larger interests are met. The sensible approach is to work directly with each other because the parties involved are best positioned to fashion a win–win solution. Thus, conflict is turned into a source of creative ideas and a way for people to strengthen their esprit de corps.

Why do people see conflict as bad while others think it is good? As Berns explains in his book *Iconoclast: A Neuroscientist Reveals How to Think Differently*, we carry with us a mental model that determines how we interpret and react to what happens around us. And this is happening unconsciously all the time. Can we modify this mental model?

Why Do You Work?

Work means a different set of experiences to each one of us. And how we view work will be dependent on the mental model that we have mentioned. Most people work because they have to: they need to earn a living. A small proportion of people work because they enjoy what they are doing. Within this segment, an even smaller number of individuals will say that their work affords them a sense of purpose and meaning. It is their calling.

People who work only for the money see work as a means to an end. It doesn't excite them. They may not slack, but what they do is geared towards ensuring that they get to keep their job. In other words, they will not go the extra mile.

People who love what they are doing are the most motivated and productive. They are usually highly enthusiastic and willing to take on challenges that others may avoid. To many people a difficult assignment is a thankless task. But for people who find purpose and meaning in their work, it is an opportunity to stretch themselves further and add value to their environment. It is also an opportunity for growth.

Work as a Calling

Let's examine the concept of work as a calling in the following cases.

Case 1

ANTON CORP was the world's leading maker of mobile phones. It was started 20 years ago by Terry J., a young technopreneur, who had a vision to transform the mobile communications market through innovative wireless solutions. By integrating hardware, software and services that supported multiple wireless-network standards, Anton offered users access to information and data via email, phone, texting, the Internet and any desired intranet-based applications. They literally created a new category for mobile communications: the smart phone.

CHAPTER 4

Part Two

Their products were an instant hit. Anton grew spectacularly, and was immensely profitable in the years ahead. It soon became one of the world's most admired companies. Terry J. was a visionary and charismatic leader. He had an opinion on almost everything which he would share freely. And he didn't suffer fools gladly. He knew that to keep at the cutting edge, talent would be key. Given the company's reputation, many of the industry's best and brightest were soon working in Anton.

Since the inception of the company, the business environment had been rapidly changing, but the company seemed frozen in its track. Even at its height of success, there were signs that the trend was towards what could be called the consumerization of information technology. This was counter to the business-to-business (B2B) business model of the company which was to design and market to businesses, i.e. people who ran corporate information-technology departments.

The rise of social media hit Anton like a bolt from the blue. Its drop was precipitous and merciless when the iPhone, Samsung Galaxy, Android, mobile phone apps and the tablets arrived. For a number of years before the guillotine fell, there were a few farsighted managers who approached Terry J. and his executive leadership team to share their views about emerging consumer and technological trends, i.e. the rise of the business-to-consumer (B2C) business space. Terry J. responded pointedly that they were misreading market signals. These were all fads that would soon die a natural death. There was no need to change course. In his inimitable tone, he warned: "Don't go barking up the wrong tree. Have faith. We must remain true to our mission."

Despite mounting hostility from the brass, a couple of fearless individuals persisted. Two years later, when the top leaders finally wised up, it was too late. Overnight, Anton crashed from its Olympian heights. Today, Anton has a new CEO. It is desperately trying to resuscitate itself through a new technology platform that targets the hyperconnected users and transforms mobile communications to true mobile computing.

Case 2

Mention **SINGAPORE**, and many people around the world will be reminded of its ban on chewing gum and the caning incident of an American schoolboy. These are trivial incidents that happened decades ago. Since its independence about 50 years ago, the country has come very far. Around the world, Singapore is recognized as a small nation that has become successful through sheer hard work, a can-do spirit and a pragmatic and honest government that inspires the people to unite and create a future against overwhelming odds. It is held up by many as a great exemplar of an agile entrepot in a turbulent world economy, a smart city in an age where sustainable urbanization is of paramount importance, and a pioneering info-state in an era where data coexist with democracy to ensure sound governance. It is also one of the most liveable cities in the world, and a strategic location in which multinationals prefer to set up their regional headquarters.

Part Two CHAPTER 4

Today, Singapore is at an inflection point. It now has a new generation of citizens born into affluence and does not know much about hardship and thriftiness. The literacy rate is among the highest in the world. Singaporeans are well travelled and plugged into the latest happenings around the world 24/7. The government consists of top officials who are earmarked on the basis of their academic brilliance. Such people are awarded scholarships that take them to the best universities in the world, particularly in the United States. Upon their return, they rise quickly up the bureaucracy to head the various government agencies. Such policy makers take the technocratic approach in governing Singapore.

Singapore continues to be well run, and is the envy of much of the world. But the last few years have seen a stirring of unrest and dissatisfaction that is completely unprecedented in its history. People, especially the younger ones, are angry and speaking up. More and more members of the opposition are getting voted into parliament. A whole host of social concerns are surfacing such as public transportation, housing, healthcare, university education, the aging work force, living cost, declining birth-rate, immigration, fear of loss of competitiveness, etc. The recent White Paper on Population was a lightning rod. This led to a rancorous nationwide debate.[2]

Citizens, pundits and other observers have weighed in on what is happening. The general consensus is that the government has not reinvented itself to keep pace with the needs and expectations of a changing Singapore landscape. Many are saying that the political leaders and the top civil servants are elitist and out of touch with the people. Only the *crème de la crème* makes it to the ranks of Singapore's top public service leaders. When these elites are assembled, diversity is noticeably missing. Everyone possesses impeccable academic credentials. They are so alike in temperament, behaviour, perspectives, and even dress alike. Virtually all are left-brained thinkers!

What is causing all the misses and policy missteps? The nation's highest public offices require leaders who possess street smarts and character above all. Scholastic record is an incomplete measure of intellectual aptitude. All it says is that the individual has a knack for acing exams and assessments, i.e. exam smarts as opposed to street smarts.

Many high-flying government leaders have expressed privately that they have grave misgiving with some policies that are being rolled out. Yet, they admit that they don't speak up as they fear dissent will not be welcomed. When Singapore first became independent, its first generation of political leaders comprised people who had a sense of mission: to breathe life into an accidental nation that few thought would survive. They dreamt big, ventured into uncharted waters and created a bustling metropolis that is the envy of many nations around the world. They had a calling.

Part Two CHAPTER 4

Our Freedom to Choose

World-renowned psychiatrist Viktor Frankl[3] spent many years in the most horrendous of conditions in Nazi concentration camps during World War II. Despite suffering unspeakable horror and cruelty, he survived. He went on to author the classic *Man's Search for Meaning*. He was also the founder of humanistic medicine and logotherapy, which seeks to make us aware that we all possess the freedom of response to all aspects of our destiny. In short, Frankl's essential teaching[4] is:

> *Between stimulus and response, there is a space. In that space lies our freedom and our power to chose our response. In our response lies our growth and happiness.*

Earlier on we discussed that we have our own peculiar way of interpreting reality. It becomes our learned thinking pattern. In effect, through repeatedly defaulting to such a style of thinking and behaviour, we create neural pathways in our brain. Then our responses become automatic, and soon the way we think and behave seems to be beyond our control. We become prisoners of our own thoughts.

As Frankl showed through his life and teachings, we need not, and should not, allow ourselves to remain an inmate in our self-created prison. We can choose to see situations differently and thereby find greater meaning and purpose in what we are doing.

As discussed earlier, people who see conflict as negative and withdraw into their silos are prisoners of their own thoughts. Ditto for the government bigwigs who do not speak up because they are fearful that doing so will be career limiting. We also saw people who refuse to be held hostage by their thoughts: those who view conflicts positively, and the few courageous people in Anton Corp who laboured courageously, albeit in vain, to save their company.

We all have a choice. It is up to us to exercise it. That requires character, conviction, courage and wisdom. There will be risks involved. But what worthy undertaking carries no risk? The reward is the meaning that comes from serving a larger cause. In a seminal article in *Harvard Business Review* entitled "How Will You Measure Your Life?" Clayton M. Christensen[5] advised that we should not be overly concerned about our own level of prominence. Rather, we should be asking whether we have helped others to become better in the course of our work and life. His final recommendation is this:

> *Think about the metric by which your life will be judged and make a resolution to live every day so that in the end, your life will be judged a success.*

CHAPTER 4

Part Two

In Chapter 5, we will discuss how leaders help individuals become better people.

PRACTICES

Q1: What is the single biggest reason you are doing what you are doing?

Q2: The strategy that the bosses (including yourself) have endorsed isn't working out. Everybody knows this. But no one wants to raise the red flag. What will you do?

PEOPLE
ARE THE BEST INVESTMENT

If you want one year of prosperity, cultivate grains.
If you want ten years of prosperity, cultivate trees.
If you want one hundred years of prosperity, cultivate people.

Confucius (551–479 BC)
Chinese philosopher

A lot of managers will say readily that people are the key to the success of their organizations. Yet, if you ask them how much time they spend on people matters, the answer is rather stunning: very little.

By force of habit, leaders tend to separate *work* from *people* issues. They will devote nearly all attention to work, and will deal with people only when they have to, i.e. when it has become a bit of a problem. Blame it on our results-oriented mentality. By focusing on work directly, leaders receive a sense of instant gratification. The reasoning goes like this. Time is scarce. We have so many things to handle. Thus, to get tangible returns quickly, we should focus all our energy on work itself.

When people issues are of a much lower priority in leaders' agenda, the upshot is a sense of disengagement that pervades workforces globally. The 2012 Towers Watson Global Workforce Study[1] provides a comprehensive assessment of this state of affairs. It covered more than 32,000 employees that represented the populations of full-time employees working in large and midsize organizations across a range of industries in 29 markets around the world. Towers Watson categorized the employees into four distinct engagement segments:

1. *Highly engaged (35 per cent):* Such employees willingly do what it takes to help their organizations succeed.
   They feel enabled by their direct-line supervisors and are energized by a work environment that supports physical, emotional and interpersonal well-being.

2. *Unsupported (22 per cent):* These people are committed to their job but lack enablement and energy for complete engagement.

3. *Detached (17 per cent):* Such employees feel supported and/or energized but aren't willing to go the extra mile.

4. *Disengaged (26 per cent):* These people feel neglected and disconnected from their workplace. They will do the minimum to get by. Most of them will slack on the job.

The study shows that globally, only just a third of employees are highly engaged, while two-thirds, the overwhelming majority, are feeling unsupported, detached or completely disengaged. This does not augur well for organizations. Given that there is a strong

correlation between strong company performance and high levels of engagement, what this means is that there is a vast reservoir of energy, ideas and productivity that is either lying dormant or negatively impacting the people in organizations.

This is a wake-up call. The results of the 2012 Towers Watson Study aren't unique. Although other survey companies reported their engagement results differently, one thing is consistent: the proportion of engaged people pales in comparison with the remaining two-thirds of the employees. And this trend has not changed much during the last few decades!

People Are Leaders' Job 1

What would leaders give to convert some of the massive two-thirds of dormant and negative energies? There are a few key drivers. First and foremost, leaders must recognize that people are their job 1.

Renowned management thinker Peter Drucker[2] once advised a CEO:

> *Your first role ... is the personal one. It is the relationship with people, the development of mutual confidence, the identification of people, the creation of a community. This is something only you can do ... It cannot be measured, or easily defined. But it is not only a key function. It is one only you can perform.*

There are countless examples that attest to the saying, *"People first, performance and results will follow"*. If by focusing on people we get improved results, why not? Sounds like a no-brainer, most of us will say. Yet, if we look at organizational key performance indicators (KPI), tangible and measurable results are all over the place. Where is the evidence that people are leaders' job 1?

CHAPTER 5

Part Two

To be realistic, no leader survives if he does not take care of today's business needs. These are non-negotiable challenges that must be addressed. This is where leaders get their sense of instant gratification. However, beyond existential requirements, all organizations aspire to be flourishing in the years ahead. Whose job is it to prepare for the future? Not those managers who define their role as minding business needs and protecting their career. This will be left to the rare individuals to whom leadership is a privilege and a calling. They will do this because they want to. But as Drucker alluded, it can neither be measured nor defined. Such leaders see their responsibilities as three-fold:

- Picking the right people.
- Creating an environment to bring out the best in people.
- Laying the foundation for the future, come what may.

Create a People-Centred Culture

In Chapter 3, we discussed the case of Vineet Nayar.[3] When he was made president of the Delhi-based IT services provider HCL Technologies, the IT service industry was changing rapidly. HCL was losing its attractiveness as it had become an undifferentiated service provider. Customers preferred a business partner that could offer end-to-end services. Nayar turned his company around within five years. Sharing his reflection, he wrote that it wasn't he who did it. The credit should go to his 100 senior managers and 55,000 employees who brought about the transformation. All he did was to speak the truth as he saw it. He then offered ideas, told stories, asked questions and even danced. Most importantly, he led by example.

It was a counterintuitive approach. Conventional management thinking would declare customers first. Without customers, there

would not be us, as the saying goes. Nayar instead started a revolution in HCL by putting employees first and customers second. How did he come to such a bold leap of faith? In his initial weeks, he travelled extensively around the world meeting with employees and also customers. What struck him in his discussions with customers was that they didn't talk much about HCL's products, services or technologies. They spoke about HCL's employees. Nayar realized quickly that the key to greatness was in the intersection between the customers and HCL's frontline employees. Imagine what value would be unleashed if employees knew they came first and felt empowered!

Another outstanding example is Zappos. Zappos is an American online shoes and apparel store founded by Tony Hsieh,[4] an entrepreneur with a computer science degree from Harvard. In the early years, their biggest problem was customer service — specifically finding the right employees to staff their call centre. Outsourcing their call centre to India or elsewhere was quickly ruled out as an option. Zappos is today a multibillion-dollar online company based in Las Vegas known best for their customer service, free shipping and 365-day return policy. Tony Hsieh attributes their phenomenal growth to their investment in terms of money, time and resources in three key areas: customer service, company culture and employee training and development.

In his book *Delivering Happiness: A Path to Profits, Passion and Purpose*, he explains that when employees are happy, they go on to do great things for the company and themselves. He boils happiness down to four factors: empowerment, perceived progress, connectedness (meaning the number and depth of your relationships) and being part of something larger than yourself. He adds that employees who become part and parcel of Zappos really need to believe in the company's long-term vision and feel at one with the culture. Therefore, before saying *Yes!* to joining the company, they are encouraged to talk to their friends and family and ask themselves: "Is this a company I really believe in? Is this a culture I really want to be part of and contribute to?"

Both Zappos and HCL turned management thinking on its head. Deep down, their leaders stumbled on a deep truth:

> *If you want the best from your people, treat them with care and respect. If people know they are first in the eyes of their company, they will in turn put customers first!*

Lead by Example

A company culture is organic and will evolve continuously. When the leaders and the people in the organization behave in a manner consistent with the values espoused, the culture becomes an enabler for high performance. On the other hand, if the values and the daily actions at the company are completely disconnected, cynicism and negativity will result. Here are some questions to consider:

- If people are said to be at the heart of the company, how much time do leaders spend with people?
- What is the quality of relationship and interaction at the top? This sets the tone for the whole company.
- If collaboration is important, how much weight does it receive when deciding on reward and recognition?
- If openness is encouraged, how is information disseminated?
- How inclusive do people feel?
- If people's ideas are valued, how safe is it for dissonant ideas to be voiced?

CHAPTER 5

Part Two

- If mistakes are made in the course of experimentation, what will be the consequences?
- How is diversity manifested and encouraged?
- If integrity is a core value, in a crisis, how do leaders behave?

Pick the Right People and Develop Them

Leaders like Tony Hsieh will first ensure that the people they recruit are right for their companies. This is a crucial first step. Then on an ongoing basis, they will invest in their development. Not just the high-potentials but everyone else. The most effective form of development is for managers to devote time one-on-one with their people by coaching, giving feedback, listening and asking questions.

The best way for people to upgrade themselves is to do it on the job and gain experience. Good judgement comes from experience, and experience comes from bad judgement. Thus, they create a safe environment to experiment, fail, learn and succeed. There are four compelling reasons for you as a manager to coach your people:

- It is a social responsibility of all managers to invest in developing their people. Managers are part of a privileged group with immense impact on people around them. By passing on their learning, they contribute to a better workplace and society.
- It raises the capabilities of your people. When they become successful, you become successful.
- You develop a reputation as a people developer and will become a magnet for talent. Talented people gravitate towards leaders who groom and develop their staff.

- You will have more time to focus on higher value-added activities. This is how you can make a more impactful contribution to your organization.

Share Learning and Meaning

People all seek meaning in their work. They are keen to understand more of the context and challenges that their company is operating in. When they are better informed, they feel honoured and respected as valuable members of their community. It touches something deep in them because they are participating in creating and sharing meaning and a larger purpose.

Wise leaders conduct sharing sessions[5] with their people so that senior executives and employees learn from each other. It creates a context for trust and relationship to be forged. In such a setting, leaders openly provide information about the progress of the company — not only the ups but also the downs. Some will share stories of what they have learnt, as well as mistakes made. In one company, one leader spoke about the importance of ensuring that people who are recruited have the right kind of values apart from possessing the competencies required. His talk was entitled, "Recruitment is like selecting a son-in-law".

It is also an opportunity to talk about the future of the company in the context of an increasingly complex and unpredictable world. Hearing about customer feedback and the impact on them and their lives makes customer satisfaction the *raison d'etre*. This is a major investment in time and energy. Not many leaders are willing to do this. The returns are difficult to quantify. In time, a community of learning will evolve. Both the leaders and their people will become wiser, more confident of each other and vested in the success of the company.

Be Curious and Humble

In our complex world, only those who are insatiably curious and keen to learn will be able to reinvent themselves and be innovative. Leaders should be exemplars of this quality. Do they ask questions or tell? Do they welcome contrarian views? How do they keep improving themselves? Do they admit it when they don't know? Can they learn from their peers and subordinates?

Leaders who stay curious and keep learning new things set the climate for others to do likewise. There is an air of intellectual excitement. It sets off a virtuous learning spiral. Knowledge begets more knowledge. Innovation and creativity follow. In the next chapter, we will discuss how leaders raise everybody's game.

PRACTICES

Q1: Do you believe in the saying, "People first, performance and results will follow"? How measurable is this leadership philosophy?

Q2: How do you identify the right people for your team? What difficult choices will you make to ensure you have a great team?

Q3: How do you engender a love of learning in your company?

Chapter 6

RAISING EVERYBODY'S
GAME

*Limited by space, a frog in the well has no idea
what is the ocean.
Limited by time, an insect in summer has no idea what is ice.
Limited by intellect, a man in life has no idea
what is Consciousness.*

Zhuang Zi (369–286 BC)[1]
Chinese Daoist

Organizations around the world are constantly trying to raise productivity and stimulate creativity as cost is rising and competitors are gaining on them. The usual focus areas are process improvements, automation and encouraging collaboration. However, companies have missed out completely on one particular area. This chapter will discuss how by unleashing the hidden potential of their people at all levels, there will be a surge in creativity and productivity. Yet, this is outside the awareness of most leaders in organizations.

The Frog in the Well

In the folklores of China and India, there is a cautionary tale of the frog in the well that holds valuable lessons for leaders in the modern age. *Frog in the Well* is known as *kupamanduka* in Sankrit. The story goes like this:

Once there was a frog that lived in a well. He was so happy with his home as he thought that it was the whole world. He jumped around happily and felt superior to the wriggly worms, crabs and tadpoles at his feet.

One day, a turtle from the sea came visiting. From the top of the well, the turtle looked in and heard the frog bragging, "I am lord of this well and I stand tall here. My happiness is great. My dear sir, why don't you come more often and look around my place?"

The turtle then told the frog about the sea and the bigger world outside the well. After listening to these words, the frog of the shallow well was shocked into realization of his own insignificance and became very ill at ease.

Unique Value-Added at Every Level

In most organizations, especially in large multinationals and government agencies, there is a deep hierarchy. Typically, there are up to six to seven levels in descending order as follows:

- Level 7: CEO or enterprise manager
- Level 6: Group manager

- Level 5: Business manager
- Level 4: Functional manager
- Level 3: Manager of managers
- Level 2: First-line manager
- Level 1: Individual contributors

The trend these days is towards flatter organizations. However, it is unlikely that hierarchy will disappear anytime soon. Why have hierarchy in the first place? In large organizations, it is neither possible nor practical for all decisions to be taken by one person at the top. Having different levels will allow matters of lesser importance to be devolved down the ranks. This will then enable the more senior people to focus on more strategic matters.

For hierarchy to serve its purpose, the role and value at every level must be well defined with minimal overlapping between layers. What is the reality in practice? Ask Ram Charan, a renowned business adviser, author and speaker who has spent the past 35 years working with many top companies, CEOs and boards. In the book *The Leadership Pipeline*,[2] Charan and his colleagues observe that

> in many companies, at least 50 per cent of leaders at various levels are operating far below their assigned layer.

In numerous talks that I gave, when I raised this topic many in the audience would nod their heads in agreement. This means that despite being elevated up the rungs, many leaders aren't pulling their weight and fulfilling their potential. Worse, they are clogging up the system by stifling the growth of their subordinates. Put it in another way, most leaders aren't adding value that is appropriate to their levels. There are two underlying reasons:

CHAPTER 6

Part Two

1. Most organizations do a poor job preparing people for higher responsibilities. Typically, at the lower levels, what get valued are technical skills that produce operational results. However, at higher levels, the responsibilities are more complex and will require a broader repertoire of competencies. But most people who are promoted lack such skills. As the saying goes, to a hammer, everything looks like a nail. Hence, they will deal with all challenges as technical issues. Frequently, when their subordinates seek help from them, they are quick to provide solutions instead of encouraging them to accept ownership of their rightful responsibilities.

2. At higher levels, the value that a leader should add is not that well defined or even quantifiable. There is also much interdependence with other colleagues' objectives. Most managers aren't comfortable with this fuzziness. Under pressure, they will do what comes naturally, i.e. take charge and take action without fully considering the ramifications of what they do. This may frequently result in other complications as the needs, perception and deeply ingrained mindset of other stakeholders have not been addressed.

Thus, it is common to see senior executives micromanaging subordinates. In addition, they are quick to prescribe a rather fragmented approach to tackling complex issues, ignoring deeper causes which continue to fester. In effect, instead of adding value they are destroying value as:

- They stifle and frustrate their subordinates by usurping their jobs.

- They can't see the larger picture because they are constantly caught in the thick of action.
- They can't influence and mobilize others to work towards a common cause.

Now imagine an organization in which:

- Leaders consciously focus on what is expected at their levels. They will empower and give work back to their subordinates.
- Leaders pause regularly to view and reflect on wider patterns emerging in the environment. They will engage and mobilize others to collectively understand new challenges and be part of the solution.

In such a company, everyone's game is raised. Leaders bring a sense of perspective, calmness and purpose. People feel engaged and included. When people are empowered, they will give more of themselves to the work. Quantum leaps in productivity follow.

The Rise and Fall and Rise Again of a Company

In the story of the frog in the well, the frog initially had no sense of how large the world was. His worldview was decidedly circumscribed because he was sitting at the bottom of the well. But when he jumped out of it, a much larger world awaited him. Finding himself out of his comfort zone, he would have to pick up new skills and adapt. Or else.

Let's now look at how *the frog in the well syndrome* pervaded the ranks of a global electronic contract manufacturer.

In the early 1990s, **RAND ELECTRONICS SYSTEMS** was one of the world's largest electronic contract manufacturers with factories in various parts of the world. Their customers owned some of the world's best-known brands in printers, desktop computers, laptops, high-end hi-fi systems, pacemakers, etc.

It had been founded by an engineer. The start-up grew rapidly with funding from venture capitalists. Within two years, numerous manufacturing sites were added rather haphazardly. Soon, it was obvious that the founder was out of his depth as he had little management expertise. The company had become unwieldy, and complaints about service and quality from key accounts were mounting.

On the board of directors was Arun, a recently retired venture capitalist. He brought with him a wealth of experience in technology companies and was highly respected by his fellow directors. All board members felt that Arun would make a great CEO, and help Rand find its bearings again.

Arun agreed rather reluctantly to accept the job only on the condition that he would step down as soon as the right person was found to run the business. Within 15 months, Arun had revitalized the company and turned it around. With a renewed sense of vigour and purpose, the business expanded further. Thoughts about recruiting another CEO were put on hold as the business was going great guns.

Five years vanished in a flash. Arun, already in his 60s, announced one day that he could not continue as CEO as his health was worsening. Rather hurriedly, the board reviewed the list of possible successors. Only two internal candidates stood out. The first was Gary, the chief operating officer (COO).

The other was Laurent, the senior vice president of marketing. Gary was an outstanding COO. With him as the czar of operations, the company had become consistently the most efficient and profitable in the industry. He was a well-respected leader who was able to get the best out of his people. Talent development and succession planning were his two top priorities. He also led by example and was a key driver in creating a work climate in which people felt trusted and empowered.

While Gary was clearly the preferred candidate of most of the board members, there were some who felt that Laurent, who was more unconventional and intuitive, would be a better choice. Laurent had a shorter tenure than Gary and was a little younger. But he clearly had greater insights about industry trends and had called out on a number of occasions that some leading competitors were now offering product development services in addition to contract manufacturing. They were becoming ODMs (original design manufacturers). Laurent was pushing hard to go down this route as well.

Unfortunately, most of the board members were rather sceptical about the wisdom of such a strategic shift. They argued that customers were likely to want to do their design work in-house rather than outsource this vital competency to contract manufacturers. They also felt that Rand possessed a competitive edge hard to match by others: they were arguably the most efficient and reputable in the industry. Indeed, all their facilities were running at full throttle. Why react rashly? they argued.

When the board took a vote, Gary won hands-down, and was tapped as the new president/CEO. The senior

leadership team and the workforce at large welcomed Gary's appointment to the company's highest post. In his first year as CEO, he continued to steer the company steadily. He made no changes and continued the strategy laid down by his predecessor who had left behind a proud legacy. His biggest focus was cost reduction and improving operational efficiency.

However, the business space was rapidly changing. Labour cost was rising in all countries they were operating in. The ODM trend was growing. Yet, Gary continued to focus on operational efficiency despite attempts by Laurent to persuade him to rethink their strategy. Suddenly, revenue and profitability started to decline steeply as big customers moved away from Rand towards the ODMs. Eighteen months into his tenure, the crisis had become full blown. Although Gary now finally began to see the light, he was still rather ambivalent about steering the company into uncharted waters.

The board had to make a painful decision. Gary was asked to make way for Laurent as the CEO. Under Laurent, the company went through 24 months of painful restructuring. Today, it has reinvented itself as an ODM.

Let's deconstruct what had transpired at Rand Electronics Systems at the leadership levels:

- The board of directors
- Arun, the first CEO
- Gary, the second CEO
- Laurent, the third CEO

The board of directors

One of the primary responsibilities of the board was to advise on the strategy for the business and ensure that succession planning was treated as top priority. Rand's board lacked diversity in expertise and perspectives, with most members from the banking and financial sector. It felt short on many counts, especially in succession planning and providing guidance to its CEO.

Its focus was short term. As long as the business was doing well, the members were content. They did not look far ahead and ask difficult and inconvenient questions of the CEO and his team. They lacked a sense of higher purpose, and frankly fell asleep at the switch. A particularly egregious oversight was their unwillingness to confront reality and act courageously. Those who felt that Laurent's thinking was more progressive kept their views to themselves.

Arun, the first CEO

Here was an industry veteran who reluctantly took the role of interim CEO. He did such a great job in first rescuing the company, and then taking it to greater heights. The interim engagement soon morphed into a five-year tenure. Though the company owed much to him, there were many acts of omission. He got so involved in running the company that he did not pause to look outside for emerging trends. And he clearly was unaware that as CEO it was imperative for him to peer into the future and speculate about reinventing his company for disruptive challenges that would surely come. He was also clueless about proactively identifying and preparing successors to take the company on its next lap.

As leaders step up to assume higher responsibilities, their mental model of their role and the way they make sense of the environment must evolve as well. Unfortunately, this does not always happen. Many leaders remain stuck in a level of consciousness more appropriate for a lesser role.[3]

To paraphrase Zhuang Zi, Arun was an intellectual midget who could not extricate himself from existentialism. Being the quintessential frog in the well, his all-consuming focus was unfailingly that of the custodian. He never took his hands off the steering wheel. What if he had stepped away from being in charge and looked in from the outside? Would the view now be a little nuanced and more fuzzy? What questions would creep into his consciousness?

Gary, the second CEO

As COO, Gary had a number of great qualities:

- Possessing a clear focus on operational responsibilities
- Growing and developing talented people
- Creating a high-performance team
- Playing an instrumental role in implanting a DNA of relentless pursuit of efficiency

However, he did not recognize that as CEO, his role was much larger than that of a COO, and had a higher order of complexity. He devoted all his time to the here and now.

As CEO, he should have delegated the day-to-day oversight to his senior people, so that he could peek far into the future. These were questions that he could have asked:

- What business are we in?
- Who are our customers? What value do they get from us?
- How is the business landscape changing?
- What are our competitors doing?
- What do customers value now?

- How should I add value as CEO?
- How must we reinvent ourselves?

Gary was way over his head as CEO. He cut a tragic figure because his consciousness as a leader also did not evolve in tandem with increasing responsibilities. He was hopelessly stuck in his well. The last two questions listed above never crossed his mind.

Laurent, the third CEO

Laurent was just about the only senior leader who had the ability to step back and seek perspective in the midst of action. He had a much broader definition of his role as a senior vice president. Instead of seeing it purely through the functional lens of marketing, he viewed himself both as a custodian and explorer. Hence, it was not just to manage the here and now, but also to prepare for the future. He therefore took it upon himself to keep abreast of industry trends and to try to influence his senior colleagues about the need for a new business model. He was pushing to disrupt the current business model in order to reinvent the company.

Unfortunately, he did not gain traction. It was definitely an uphill battle for Laurent, given that nearly all his senior colleagues were frogs trapped in their own wells. What could Laurent have done differently to help his bosses shift their mindset?

Get on the Balcony

In organizations, bias for action is a mantra. It is very easy and natural to get caught up in the action, especially when the companies are riding on a crest of success. While subtle signals of changes

CHAPTER 6

Part Two

are appearing in the environment, such leaders will ignore them until it is too late. Ron A. Heifetz[4] of Harvard Kennedy School has sound words of advice for leaders: *Get on the balcony!*

Imagine a big ballroom with a balcony up above. You are one of the dancers. While dancing, you will notice that the band is playing and people are swirling around to the music. Most of your attention will be reserved for your dancing partner. You will take care not to collide with other dancers. When asked how the experience is, you may say that the music is great and that everybody seems so happy.

Now go up to the balcony and look down on the dance floor. The picture will be very different. You will notice that less people dance when slow music is played. When the tempo increases more gather at the dance floor. Some people never dance at all. Later you will remark that participation is sporadic and that the band isn't able to get more people onto the dance floor.

Leaders who are constantly busy are too close to the action. They will miss larger patterns, follow dominant trends and thinking, and be blindsided by emerging patterns. Thus, it is imperative that leaders be willing to climb on the balcony regularly. And then they must go back to the dance floor so that they can engage others around them to see the new perspective. Effective leaders are able to switch back and forth from dancing and going to the balcony. Great performers, whether in the corporate, military, artistic or sports arena, do this all the time. Under stress, they are in and out of the game simultaneously.

How to Raise Everybody's Game

The work that people perform in organizations can be categorized in four areas as follows:[5]

- Key responsibilities
- Key skills
- Key stakeholders
- Value-added

As people move up from one level to the next, they will need to lead and interact differently and leave the old ways behind. They also need to acquire new skills so that increasingly they can raise the consciousness in others to a higher level.

Heifetz[6] distinguishes between technical and adaptive challenges that leaders will face. Technical challenges are easy to identify. They lend themselves to solutions by people who are experts. Though complicated, their impact is often quite well contained within organizational boundaries. Solutions can be implemented, even by edict. In contrast, adaptive challenges are difficult to identify. Even if one could define the problem, people involved might choose to deny its existence. Solutions will involve changes in values, beliefs, relationships, roles and responsibilities. Their impact will not be easily contained and will cross organizational boundaries.

The technical challenge that Rand faced initially was to consolidate its unwieldy operations and raise efficiency and productivity. This was an area that Gary excelled in as COO. Laurent faced an adaptive challenge in trying to convince his bosses to change course. When he became the CEO, the challenge of reinventing the company was both a blend of technical and adaptive challenges.

The biggest failure of leadership is to treat adaptive challenges as technical challenges. Gary as CEO failed to see the adaptive challenge that was staring him in the face. He thought it would go away if he continued to deal with it as a technical challenge by focusing on operational efficiency. As for Laurent, his attempt at convincing his bosses about the dire need to course-correct fell on deaf ears. He didn't realize that he was pushing his bosses out of their comfort zone. That was an adaptive challenge that required a lot of trust-building and lobbying.

First, he had to focus on working with Arun and Gary one-on-one, and then together as a threesome. Second, he needed to recognize that in their minds he was young and unconventional and therefore was not taken seriously. He thus had to establish his credibility and win their trust. Third, with the support of Arun and Gary, they could then approach the board and sell their vision for a new business model.

Leaders who wish to raise everybody's game have to work on themselves first. They will need to ask themselves whether they are adding value appropriate to their levels. Do they get on the balcony frequently to see emerging patterns? How are they dealing with technical and adaptive challenges?

Next, they coach their people to help them raise their game. Sharing the metaphors of the *frog in the well* and *getting on the balcony* will help to enhance people's awareness and consciousness.

PRACTICES

Q1: Does Dr Charan's observation that "at least 50 per cent of the people in leadership positions are operating far below their assigned layer" resonate with you?

Q2: What game are you playing now? How should you raise your own game?

Q3: How regularly do you get on the balcony in the course of your work? How does it help you?

PART THREE
SEEING NEW POSSIBILITIES

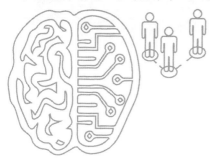

Man often becomes what he believes himself to be. If I keep on saying to myself that I cannot do a certain thing, it is possible that I may end by really becoming incapable of doing it. On the contrary, if I have the belief that I can do it, I shall surely acquire the capacity to do it even if I may not have it at the beginning.

Mahatma Gandhi (1869–1948)
father of the Indian independence movement

Chapter 7

THE WHOLE **BRAIN**

It is only with one's heart that one can see clearly;
what is essential is invisible to the eye.

Antoine de Saint-Exupery (1900–1944)
French aristocrat, writer, poet
and pioneering aviator

Scientists have long known that our brain has two regions. Until recently, the scientific establishment considered the two hemispheres as separate and unequal. The left side was always the crucial half while the right side was subsidiary. The left hemisphere made us human because it was rational, analytical and logical. The right hemisphere was redundant as it was mute, non-linear and instinctive. It was designed for the era of the hunters–gatherers that human beings had outgrown.

In the 1950s, Roger W. Sperry, a professor at the California Institute of Technology, made a startling discovery that overturned the prevailing orthodoxy about the human brain. While it had long been known that the human brain had two modes of thinking represented separately by the left and right hemispheres, Sperry now had evidence that the right brain — which scientists had thus far supposed to be subordinate and even inferior — was in fact the *superior member when it came to performing certain mental tasks.*

Since then, scientists have gone on further to understand how the two hemispheres are different. The left brain is often described as logical, sequential and literal. Its strengths are in language, critical thinking, numbers, reasoning and analysis. The right brain is better at expressive and creative activities. Its strong suits are inventiveness, empathy, emotional connection, intuition, images, music and big picture thinking.

For us to lead a fulfilling and successful life, we need to draw upon the complementary nature of both hemispheres. A useful analogy is that of an orchestra. When there are various instruments producing different sounds yet played in concert, a rich symphony is created. Contrast this with a situation where one-half of the orchestra is absent.

In his best-selling book *A Whole New Brain*, Daniel Pink[1] makes a compelling case for a more right-brain centric approach to leading and relating in the 21st century. First, he traces the progress of mankind in the last 150 years. The 19th century was the Industrial Age. The economy was powered by massive labour-intensive factories and efficient assembly lines. The leading actors were the mass production workers whose key attributes were brawn and the discipline to devote themselves to endlessly repetitive tasks.

CHAPTER 7

Part Three

Then came the Information Age in the 20th century. In the developed countries such as the United States, Western Europe and Japan, mass production was gradually receding into the background as the driver of growth. In its place, knowledge, ideas and information soon took pride of place. A new cast of characters appeared: the knowledge workers. They distinguished themselves through their sheer prowess in analysis of data and information, seeing things rationally and sequentially, logical processing and verbal skills such as talking, reading and writing. This was the province of left-brained thinking.

Knowledge workers — the engineers, scientists, accountants, doctors, lawyers and managers — defined the modern world by applying ideas, logic, systems and processes to the workplace. Engineering, modern management methods, new scientific and technological advances, networking and data processing technology soon made it possible for goods and services to be provided cost-effectively worldwide. As competition among suppliers in the West and Japan intensified, the lower value-added goods and services were outsourced to Asia. Countless jobs were created, lifting Asians to a standard of living undreamt of a generation ago. And soon millions of Asians also became schooled and trained in left-brained thinking.

And now, in the 21st century, the global economic landscape is changing dramatically again. There is a confluence of three factors: the global financial crisis emanating from the US and Euro zone countries, the shift of the centre of economic activities to Asia powered by China and India, and the rise of Asian consumerism. As Pink puts it, the forces of Abundance, Asia and Automation have arrived. He calls it the Conceptual Age.

To be sure, even as we speak, the world is still largely immersed in the Information Age. Having a huge talent pool of knowledge workers will continue to be a formidable competitive edge. However, while left-brained capabilities will remain indispensable in the Conceptual Age, the people who will occupy centre stage will be the creative types, those who excel in right-brain activities.

Why so? What the developed economies in the West can mass produce, so can the people in the East. And they can do it cheaper, faster and at equivalent consistency and quality to boot.

And within Asia itself, there is a new competitive dynamics. The developed economies such as Hong Kong, Japan, Singapore, South Korea and Taiwan are feeling the heat from not only the two Asian juggernauts China and India, but also Indonesia, Malaysia, the Philippines and Thailand. With Asia experiencing unprecedented growth, all the economies have been investing in world-class infrastructure and workforces. Gaps in capabilities are narrowing. Everybody is now jostling within the same space. None is content to be at the low end of the food chain. All aspire to move towards high-value and knowledge-intensive activities. Like surfers in the ocean, both the East and West are trying to catch the next big wave.

Catching the Next Big Wave

With rising consumerism, customers are getting increasingly spoilt for choice. In Asia, for instance, Western cosmetics and pharmaceutical companies have awakened to the fact that they can no longer foist onto Asian customers what have been traditionally developed for the West. Asians have skin types and medical conditions that are different from Caucasians'. Thus, they are investing in research labs in Asian countries and carrying out full scale Asia-based clinical and consumer trials for products specifically developed for Asian consumers. Cosmetics giant L'Oreal, for instance, has world-class research and innovation facilities in China, Japan, India and Singapore.

Functionality in a product or service is a given. Customers are now demanding artistic and emotional beauty. And everyday items such as a smart phone or a tablet computer evoke in the owner a sense of his individuality. It is a bold statement of his taste and values in pursuit of meaning and purpose.

In the Conceptual Age, creativity will be king. High-tech and left-brained qualities will still be required, but won't be sufficient. While many writers and pundits have proclaimed that the right-brainers will rule the future, in truth, creativity is a mental process that draws on both the left and right hemispheres, i.e. it is a whole-brained process.

Metaphorically speaking, left-brained activities had always been the star while right-brained thinking played the supporting role. Now a switch is taking place. Right-brained aptitudes are taking the helm, setting the course and steering the ship. It heralds the rise of creative workers. These are people who are able to view the world through the eyes of artists. Drawing upon their right-brained capabilities, they exhibit intense curiosity, view the world playfully, love to experiment and test new ideas. They are always learning, and seem to be meandering around in their pursuit of the human story in what they do. And their dabs, broad brushes and splashes on the canvas will gradually morph into a work that combines substance, style and originality.

However, lest we get carried away, the Conceptual Age is unlikely to gain traction solely by leveraging the right brain. Creative ideas will only see the light of day if evaluation, sequencing, timing,

CHAPTER 7

Part Three

planning and implementation kick in at the appropriate moment. In other words, we need to put our whole mind to work. English poet Samuel Taylor Coleridge puts it this way: *The truth is, a great mind must be androgynous.*

The Six Senses

Pink has identified six essential attributes that will enable us to leverage our whole mind at work and in life:

1. *Design.* Functionality by itself is not sufficient. Customers want both form AND substance, i.e. usefulness and beauty.

2. *Story.* If you want to win the support of your audience, data and facts won't be enough. They want all that AND an interesting narrative.

3. *Symphony.* Not just the separate pieces of the jigsaw puzzle but also the complete picture.

4. *Empathy:* People are reclaiming their humanity. They become engaged only if they are convinced that they matter to you.

5. *Play.* Work is important of course. But there is a recognition that work needs to be balanced with fun, laughter and humour.

6. *Meaning.* Millions around the world are realizing that the single-minded pursuit of wealth and possession does not lead to greater fulfilment. They seek meaning through a sense of purpose and spirituality.

In his leadership classic *On Becoming a Leader*, Warren Bennis[2] laments that:

CHAPTER 7

Part Three

❛ *a key factor that prevents capable managers from transforming themselves into successful leaders is that corporations and society place a premium on left-brain achievements and discount right-brain activities.* ❜

For instance, companies are increasingly focusing their businesses around the bottom line, return on investment, analytics and Big Data. Society at large needs to take a more balanced approach by recognizing the power of right-brained qualities such as intuition, synthesis and artistry. Bennis also observes that the outstanding people whom he interviewed — whatever their occupations — are whole-brained, capable of leveraging their intuitive and conceptual capabilities as well as their logical and analytical talents.

A Japanese Fable

Let's now examine how the left brain takes charge when we encounter an experience that is a little unexpected and bizarre. What if we had listened more to our right brain? *The Heron Maiden*[3] is an ancient Japanese story that dates back hundreds of years ago. It is richly allegorical and replete with mythical connotations.

CHAPTER 7

Part Three

One day, a young man, walking through the forest on his way home, comes upon a wounded heron. He decides to take it back with him and nurse it back to health. A few weeks later, when the heron has regained its strength, he takes it back to the woods and releases it.

Time passes, and the young man meets a beautiful young lady with whom he falls in love. They marry and begin a blissful life together. The young bride brings to their union a unique gift: her ability to weave silk brocade with ornamental designs appearing in relief. Her handiwork becomes much sought after by the people in the village. And the couple is able to support themselves through the sale of this fabric.

Something is troubling the young man though. An enigma hangs over their relationship. His wife insists that when she is weaving, he must never observe her. This is obviously a source of mystery and tension, to put it mildly. One day, unable to contain himself any longer, he steals a glance, and he beholds a heron at the loom.

Right before his eyes, the heron transforms into a beautiful young woman — his wife. The veil is lifted. An ancient pact is broken. And now, the heron's happy life with her lover must come to an end. Tearfully they bid each other farewell. The heron flies away, leaving the young man sad and mystified.

The Heron Maiden is a literary device that challenges us to pause in our track and examine the way we interpret events around us. Like all myths and folklores, it is nuanced and paradoxical, and yet deceptively simple. At a superficial level, the harried executive constantly on the go is likely to dismiss this as a case of a mismatch between two persons. Examples abound in corporate settings of partnerships that have gone awry.

If we burrow a little deeper, the tale is an object lesson on how we need to develop a new way of knowing through empathy. Subtext is what is left unspoken that the listener must fill in. In real life, we seldom speak exactly what is on our mind. The more important the topic is, the more unwilling we become to confront it head on. We will ramble on and expect others to get underneath and decode our intentions.

This is not just in Asia, where the stereotypical view about communication is that it is indirect and circumlocutory. It is the same in Europe and even in the United States. Despite being portrayed as *in your face* and *direct*, Americans, like the rest of us, are just as nuanced in their communication style on sensitive matters. How inaccurate cultural stereotypes are! In our hyperkinetic world, we have a compulsive need to see before we believe. Because of the premium placed on getting things out in the open and cutting to the chase, we frequently miss the subtlety of human interaction.

Seeing is synonymous with understanding or cognition. It is our left brain taking the driver's seat. When things are ambiguous, it muscles into our consciousness and demands for facts and data. The ancient Chinese recognized that listening is a complex process of taking in the world. When we listen through our heart, we tap into our intuition. Our overwrought mind becomes decluttered as noise and conflicting data get reconciled. And suddenly fresh insights emerge. Listening is of such importance that I have devoted the whole of Chapter 9 to it.

In the fable of *The Heron Maiden*, if the young man *listens* through his heart despite the primal temptation to *see*, how will the story end?

Taking a Whole-Brained Approach

Dorothy Leonard[4] of Harvard Business School explains the concept of cognitive differences as varying approaches to perceiving and assimilating data, making decisions, solving problems and relating to people. These approaches are preferences and should not be confused with skills or abilities.

CHAPTER 7

Part Three

She explains that managers who are successful at fostering innovation are able to engender a productive process called *creative abrasion*. They recognize that people have different thinking and behavioural preferences: analytical or intuitive, conceptual or experiential, social or independent, and logical or values-driven. Thus, in any setting such as a team, a work group or even an entire company, managers must be encouraged to drive diverse approaches and perspectives to grate against each other constructively. Only when there is respect for opposing views and styles can organizations nurture greater innovation.

There are various psychometric assessments that are helpful in understanding our cognitive and behavioural preferences. Examples are the Myer–Briggs Type Indicator (MBTI), the Herrmann Brain Dominance Instrument (HBDI) and the DISC. As a manager, how may we harness the creative energies of opposites? Here is a four-step process that has proven effective in many organizations:

1. *Understand yourself.* First identify your own style and gain insights into the ways your preferences unconsciously shape the way you lead and communicate. Also know the strengths and weaknesses of your style and how you react under pressure. Learn about other styles — their preferences, strengths and weaknesses — and appreciate how different styles may both run counter to, as well as complement, each other.

2. *Assemble a team with diverse thinking and behavioural preferences.* When assembling your team, resist selecting like-minded people. Intentionally look for people with diverse thinking and behavioural preferences. Provide an opportunity to get to know each other and understand each other's preferences.

CHAPTER 7

Part Three

3. *Value diverse opinions.* Help all members appreciate that respecting and valuing others' perspectives will enable them to examine ideas and assumptions in a more clear-eyed and unbiased manner. Though it is a more time-consuming process, the end results will be of a higher quality. In interactions, consciously ditch the Golden Rule. Don't treat others the way you wish to be treated. Instead, treat them in the way they wish to be treated. This means tailoring your messages in a way that makes most sense to the receiver. For instance, some people require lots of details, facts and figures. Others prefer the big picture, or anecdotes or stories. Some of us cringe when the notion of story-telling is broached. If we view a story as facts and data with a soul, it might suddenly become more mainstream and less touchy-feely. It should be expected that conflict will arise from time to time. Instead of suppressing it, members need to learn how to manage it constructively by depersonalizing it.

4. *Manage the creative process.* Make sure everyone speaks up and is heard and respected by the rest of the team. Have clear rules of engagement. An agenda should be explicitly set up to provide sufficient time for both divergent and convergent discussions. Then have the debate, in search of understanding. At the end of it all, don't ever expect that there will be unanimous agreement. This is when the leader earns his pay cheque. He makes the call!

In the next chapter, we will talk about paradoxes. By taking a whole-brained approach, we will experience paradoxes not as absurdities that should be dismissed but as a springboard for a deeper understanding of nature.

CHAPTER 7

Part Three

PRACTICES

Q1: What are you: left-brained or right-brained? How can you be whole-brained?

Q2: How will you handle the following situations?

Case 1

One of your managers, known to be a creative type, approaches you one day with an idea. She had been brainstorming with her team members. They suddenly had a flash of insight that they all feel will lead to a breakthrough in the market. The idea sounds a little wild to you. It is still in the early days. She is asking for some funding to flesh it out a little.

Case 2

During a meeting to discuss a particular project, many differing views are expressed about how to proceed. The four individuals who speak up all have valid and interesting perspectives. This much is clear. Everybody is engaged and committed to make the project a success. It is unlikely that you will be able to reach closure today on the next steps. But the deadline looms.

Case 3

You notice that over the years, your company has become dominated by the left-brained style. It has created an engineering culture that has worked very well so far. Indeed, there have been outstanding examples of creativity in innovative marketing and even clever product designs. But the environment is changing rapidly and you sense that more of the same will not cut it. You know intuitively that you will need new ideas or even new personalities to shake up the strong data-driven culture.

PARADOXES

How wonderful that we have met a paradox.
Now we have some hope of making progress.

Niels Bohr (1885–1962)
Danish Nobel laureate for physics, 1922

I n the previous chapter, we talked about our tendency to favour logic, data and analysis in the way we conduct our business. As *The New York Times* columnist David Brooks[1] puts it,

We've inherited a view of ourselves that we are divided selves, that we have reason over here and emotion over there. … We value things we can quantify … and we tend not to devalue, but to be inarticulate about the rest.

No one is saying that we should dispense with data and logic. This approach has served us well and will continue to do so. Yet, we need to recognize that business and human affairs do not always come in neat packages. When situations seem rather irrational, paradoxical or even absurd, will data and logic on their own help us? This will be like trying to win at a team sport like soccer using skills honed in the game of chess. By not unlearning and relearning, we will have foregone a unique opportunity to adapt and thrive in a more complex environment.

What Are Paradoxes?

Paradoxes are a reminder to us that nature works in mysterious ways. For far too long, the Western view is that the world is a mechanistic one which derives from Cartesian–Newtonian science.

According to the distinguished physicist Fritjof Capra,[2] these concepts are now outdated. The dynamics underlying the major crises of our time — social, political, ecological and cultural — emanate from this artificial and fragmented view of society. The natural environment is carved into separate parts and exploited by different interest groups. We have alienated ourselves from nature and from our fellow human beings. Capra, through a series of thought-provoking books and seminars, has called for a more holistic paradigm of science and for cultivating the human spirit. Scientists are now shifting to a holistic and ecological view, which is similar to those of mystics of all ages and traditions.

Paradoxes are curved balls that nature throws at us to get us to take pause and re-examine our approach towards meaning-making. They come in the form of a statement, proposition, situation or even a person, that seems to be self-contradictory. These elements are present: two polar opposites, mutual exclusivity and simultaneity.

CHAPTER 8

Part Three

Both claim validity thereby invoking a sense of absurdity. Our logical understanding of the world is being turned upside down. There is tension within us because the dilemma we are presented with defies logic. Here are some examples:

- To have control, you will have to give up control.
- A strength overdone becomes a weakness.
- Smart people find it difficult to learn.
- The more you do, the less you accomplish.
- Abundant resources can be a curse to a country.
- The only way to succeed is to fail again and again.
- Those who know a lot, speak very little; those who know very little, speak a lot.
- Stress is both bad and good for your body and mind.
- A person can be both good and evil.
- A crisis is an opportunity.

The Concept of Complementarity

The Eastern view of the world is *organic* in contrast with the mechanistic Western view. According to Lao Zi, all things and events in nature are interrelated, connected and are but different manifestations of the same ultimate reality. We first discussed this in Chapter 3.

Thus, there is nothing inherently good or bad about the opposites that we observe in paradoxes. In fact, the Daoists view contradictions as a necessity in life. For one to exist, it needs the other. In order to have black, you will need to have white. Otherwise, how will you know you have black?

In Daoism, the two opposing forces are commonly denoted as *yin* and *yang*. The *yin–yang* symbol (shown on the following page) consists of a circle divided into two fish-shaped halves — much

CHAPTER 8

Part Three

akin to a black dolphin with a white eye intertwining with a white dolphin with a black eye. These two halves represent the *yin* and *yang* forces coexisting permanently, each blending in with the other in a continuous cycle of change.

When faced with paradoxes, we may adopt two perspectives:

1. *The opposites are contradictions and seemingly irreconcilable.* We find ourselves on the horns of a dilemma. Tension builds up. In order to stop messing around, our impulse is to decide which is *right* and which is *wrong*. This is the *either–or approach.*

2. *The opposites though apparently in conflict are also viewed as complementary.* We hold both thoughts in constructive and dialectic tension. Between the two opposites, we see a continuum along which we may generate limitless creative ideas that contain elements of the two opposites but are superior to both. This is the *both–and approach.*

Let's now look at an example of a commonly encountered paradox in organizational life.

CHAPTER 8

Part Three

It was a very tense off-site that you had organized. Fifteen team members were present. They all knew the future of the product was hanging in the balance. Since its launch a year ago, it had been an uninterrupted string of disappointments. Yet, so much hope had been invested in it. The top brass at head office were becoming impatient. Should the plug be pulled? Or should more time be given?

Towards the end of the three-day meeting, the participants agreed options A and B were the two most practical approaches given the constraints of time and resources. But there was a dilemma. Both options couldn't be more different from each other. This wasn't surprising. You could take pride that this attested to your insistence through the years that there should always be diverse perspectives. "Divergence first, then convergence" was your team's mantra.

Looking at the options objectively, there were pros as well as cons. Both were credible and well-thought out. Yet neither was surefire. There were unknowns and risks involved. How should you and your people proceed? Would you prefer to cut to the chase and pick either of the options? While that was cleaner and more straightforward, you would be settling for a suboptimal solution, given that neither was ideal.

Alternatively, you could consider the both–and approach. You could pick the best from both while avoiding their inherent weaknesses. Or you could even consider another variation by integrating parts of both options and introducing something new. This would be messier and take more time. But it could be a more robust approach.

Paradoxes Make Us Pause and Reflect

Because paradox distorts the view of the world as an objective and orderly place, we would rather not deal with it. Ilya Prigogine,[3] the 1977 Nobel laureate for physical chemistry, argued that in eliminating paradox, scientists will miss what is right in front of them, that there is both order and disorder at the same time.

To Niels Bohr's point, we owe a debt of gratitude to paradoxes. They shatter our simplistic view of nature. Now we must come to terms with the real world.

Paradoxes Stimulate Creativity

Albert Rothenberg, an expert on creative thinking, coined the term *Janusian thinking* to describe the characteristics of creative people. They have the knack of conceiving and coalescing simultaneously two or more opposing concepts. In a flash of genius, these antithetical elements fall into place in an apparent defiance of logic. Now it all makes sense!

Janus, a Greek god, is often portrayed as a man with two heads, each facing opposite directions. This is a symbol of embracing a dual perspective. In our modern world, we will need to extend this capability even further to consider multiple perspectives simultaneously.

The brilliant English scientist Michael Faraday was a self-educated and humble man. His work spanned 60 years and made him one of the giants of science in the 19th century. His discovery of the electric motor and the generator is a great example of his power to embrace paradoxes. Faraday had observed that when a compass was placed near to a wire passing an electric current,

its magnetized needle would deflect in a rotational direction. This resulted in his invention of the electrical motor.

He didn't stop there. He took a flight of fancy and wondered: "If an electric current can make magnets move, maybe a moving magnet can cause electricity to flow." Thus was born the dynamo or the electric generator. Faraday's leap of imagination is an exemplar of another great insight from Niels Bohr:

> *There are two kinds of truth, small truth and great truth. You recognize a small truth because its opposite is a falsehood. The opposite of a profound truth is another profound truth.*

Paradoxes Raise Us to a Higher Level of Understanding

Whether we are aware or not, we all settle into a fixed pattern of thinking very early in our adulthood. Like fish swimming in water who are not aware of the water around them, we stop thinking about the way we think. We have become prisoners of well-worn routines created and reinforced by past successes. A paradox throws us off our balance. Suddenly we are on the back foot. There is a sense of disbelief, a recognition that we are feeling conflicted and unsure of ourselves. How can we transcend this sense of tension and inadequacy?

Many of the world's most compelling works of arts captivate and fascinate us because they portray the theme of paradox in their inestimable fashion.[4] It is not explicit on the canvas, because artists are masters of the implicit. In Da Vinci's *Mona Lisa*, we have a perfect expression of paradox. Her mysterious half-smile is a juxtaposition of good and evil, happiness and sadness, and seduction and innocence.

In musical compositions, the audience experiences a feeling of uncomfortable closure when musicians do not play the final one chord in the two-five-one sequence. It is the silence between notes to create the dramatic tension that makes the piece powerful.

The language and structure of a poem is often indecipherable, as though the poet is bent on frustrating our senses. We are intrigued. We don't quite get it even though we read it again and again. There is a kernel of truth tucked away. The paradox is wrapped within complexity and irony, and only through reflection and abandonment of conventional logic will we achieve intuitive enlightenment.

Only those with the right sensibilities will get it. Here are two illustrations. The first one is T.S. Eliot's *East Coker* from his *Four Quartets*:[5]

> I said to my soul, be still, and wait without hope
> … … … … … … … … … … … … … …
> Wait without thought, for you are not ready for thought.
> So the darkness shall be light, and the stillness the dancing.

In the second example, most readers will have come across this rather enigmatic observation from Lao Zi:

> Those who speak, do not know;
> those who know, do not speak.

Tao Qian[6] (AD 365–427) was one of China's greatest poets and a noted recluse. In his famous poem *Drinking Wine*, while waxing lyrical about solitude and nature he laments that words fail him. Yet he knows that he knows. Thus,

In all these things there is a deep meaning,
but when we're about to express it,
We suddenly forget the words.

Companies that Thrive by Embracing Paradoxes

Toyota

When we think of Toyota, what springs to mind is its famed Toyota Production System (TPS).[7] It is the TPS that has enabled the Japanese giant to make the world's best automobiles at the lowest cost and to develop new models quickly. But this is only part of the story. While the TPS epitomizes hard innovation, there is a softer side to its unparallel success. It is the soft innovation that is related to its corporate culture.

According to Japanese professors Hirotaka Takeuchi, Emi Osono and Norihiko Shimizu, who did a six-year study of Toyota, it is contradictions that drive Toyota's success. In their own words,

The company succeeds, we believe, because it creates contradictions and paradoxes in many aspects of organizational life. Employees have to operate in a culture where they constantly grapple with challenges and problems and must come up with fresh ideas. That's why Toyota constantly gets better.

The hard and the soft innovations work like *yin* and *yang* in creating a dynamic tension between contradictions: stable and paranoid, systematic and experimental, formal and frank.

Part Three CHAPTER 8

Samsung, Haier, Infosys and Koc

Samsung[8] of South Korea, Haier of China, Infosys of India and Koc of Turkey are successful globalizers from emerging economies. What do they have in common? It is each of these giants' ability to reinvent to better position themselves for the world market. To do so, they abandon what had made them phenomenally successful in their home market and adopt new, even alien thinking and practices that seem contradictory to their culture.

Take Samsung. Twenty years ago, it was a low-cost original equipment manufacturer. Today, it is a world leader in research and development, marketing and design, with a brand name more valuable than Pepsi, Nike or American Express. As an example, its Galaxy line of smart phones and tablets are a favourite around the world and is threatening to overtake Apple. What has propelled Samsung's meteoric rise? Again, it is the juxtaposition of different sets of thinking, practices and cultures that are contradictory and seemingly incompatible. Chairman Lee Kun-Hee created a unique hybrid management system that mixed Western best practices with an essentially Japanese business system in a Korean company.

Learning How to Benefit from Paradoxes

Warren Bennis has said that it is the mechanistic view that produces the organization man, and it is the organization man who ironically causes many of the problems in our organizations. Continuing, he said:

> It is the individual, operating at the peak of his creative and moral powers who will revive our organizations, by reinventing himself and them. ... Our culture needs more right-brained qualities, needs to be more intuitive. Conceptual, synthesizing and artistic.

CHAPTER 8

Part Three

Management is a liberal art, Peter Drucker[9] said. *Liberal* because it deals with the fundamentals of knowledge, self-knowledge, wisdom and leadership; *art* because it is practices and application. There is much that philosophy, history, literature and the fine arts can help us learn to lead better. Because leadership is about people. And in the human condition we will encounter mystery, paradoxes, dilemmas, magic, wonder and fulfilment. In 1997, Drucker wrote to a friend: "I'm rereading each summer — and for many years — the main novelists." Among them were Jane Austen, William Makepeace Thackeray, Anthony Trollope and George Eliot. Then he added:

> *I never read management books. All they do is corrupt the style.*

In Chapter 9, we explore a much under-utilized gift that nature has bestowed upon us. Through deep listening, we tap into a shared wisdom and understanding that takes us to a higher level of creativity.

CHAPTER 8

Part Three

PRACTICES

Q1: Can you think of a paradoxical situation that you have encountered? What did you feel initially? How did you finally come to terms with it?

Q2: How will you encourage people at work to view paradoxes as stimuli for creative ideas?

Q3: Do you take an active interest in philosophy, history, literature and the fine arts? What have they got to do with leadership and creativity?

Q4: Revisit Chapter 3: The Light and the Shadow. What are the common themes in Chapters 3 and 8?

Chapter 9

DEEP **LISTENING**

*Listening is a magnetic and strange thing, a creative force.
The friends who listen to us are the ones we move towards.
When we are listened to, it creates us,
makes us unfold and expand.*

Karl A. Menninger (1893–1990)
American psychiatrist

Recently I sat in at a meeting of senior leaders of a consumer products company. It was their quarterly strategy review chaired by the CEO. At this particular session, there were a couple of executives who were scheduled to share their ideas on business development and HR. The executives, Kayla and Geraldine, were very alike in many ways. Both knew their subject matter very well. They were dynamic, persuasive and able to put their points across very crisply.

Kayla caught my attention quickly. During the meeting, especially when others were speaking, she was highly engaged. She listened patiently, raising clarifying questions occasionally and making thoughtful suggestions. But it seemed that when it was her turn to present her case, it was a different Kayla up there. The presentation part went perfectly. Then came the Q&A. It was at first an animated conversation, with ideas and suggestions coming from everybody. As the discussions continued, it became obvious that Kayla wasn't really listening. She was more intent on further advocating her ideas. An hour later, people were getting uncomfortable and a little frustrated. An awkward silence had descended like a suffocating veil. The CEO noticed it, and diplomatically suggested breaking for lunch. Kayla had recently been promoted to the post of vice president of business development. It was natural that she was anxious to hit the ground running. That perhaps had caused her to misinterpret the ideas and input from colleagues as challenges that she had to fend off.

It was a stark contrast from the way Geraldine, vice president of human resources, had conducted herself earlier on. She was open and relaxed during the Q&A. The conversation was free-flowing. There were ideas and comments that she readily accepted. Sometimes, she explained why she wasn't in favour of certain changes that were brought up. The topic of compensation and benefits would be a controversial one in any setting. Yet, at the end of two hours, people continued to feel engaged and included. Geraldine was quite pleased. There were only a couple of areas that she had to tweak before implementing the new scheme.

Listening Is a Critical Skill

How could Kayla have gained the goodwill and support of her senior colleagues at her maiden presentation? Like many people in organizations, she had a misguided notion about the relationship between listening and speaking in communication. When someone else was presenting, she was relaxed and generous, giving her undivided attention and chiming in constructively. But, the moment she took centre stage, she seemed to have flipped the off-switch on listening. Speaking and listening in her mind had become mutually exclusive.

If Kayla had taken pause and become more mindful of the dynamics that day, she would have been thankful for her colleagues' active participation. Ironically, in many organizations, especially those operating in silos, the more usual reaction from colleagues will be one of passivity. The mindset will be as follows:

> *If it isn't directly in my portfolio, it is best that I say less. I assume she knows what she is doing, and I don't want to come across as encroaching into her territory.*

If others had not offered their opinions, would that have given her comfort? Would the CEO have felt that Kayla's ideas had been sufficiently scrubbed from various angles and had received the support of all in the senior team? Obviously not. Senior leaders of companies have to consciously balance two roles: actively ensuring that they collectively steer the company in the right direction, and leading their respective functions effectively in collaboration with other functions. By listening openly,[1] the following benefits would have accrued to Kayla:

1. *Input from many different perspectives.* Some ideas might even be disruptive and required her to go right back to the drawing board. But which is better? To do a few more iterations and then have a more robust plan? Or to rush into implementation with a half-baked idea?

2. *Enrol her colleagues as stakeholders.* When others provide input, they are giving us their time and opinions. While we aren't obligated to accept all that is offered, humble and wise leaders recognize that when we weave others' ideas into our plan, they become co-owners in the undertaking.

3. *Build relations and mutual respect.* When we listen to others, we are saying to them that we respect them and would like to learn from them. People are sensitive. They may wish to help and may have much to offer that will advance our project or even our career. But when they sense that they aren't being listened to, they will withdraw from the engagement, as Kayla might have noticed. When a relationship starts off on a wrong footing, repairing it will be an arduous process.

Becoming a Better Listener[2]

Here are five steps that will help us to listen better.

1. Show respect to the other party

The higher one goes up in an organization, the more out of touch one may become. The expression *loneliness at the top* is very real. In fact, you don't really need to be the top leader to feel isolated. Even middle managers can be cut off from reality. But it may be their own doing, consciously or unconsciously.

With increasing responsibilities, it is a challenge keeping abreast of important happenings. And it is wise to recognize that the people down the ranks are closer to the action. They are more likely to tell you what is happening than the senior people

CHAPTER 9

Part Three

reporting directly to you. But it is unlikely that they will speak up unless they feel that you respect them and believe that they have something useful to contribute. Initially, people will be cagey. This shouldn't be surprising. The mutual trust and rapport have yet to be established.

Over time, as they get more comfortable and are convinced of your sincerity, they will be a rich source of advice and input. Leaders who make it a point of reaching out to people throughout the organization are sending a powerful message: everyone matters. When senior leaders lead by example, other leaders at various levels will follow. This will help create an environment where people feel empowered. Ideas will flow more freely in such an organization. The American essayist, poet and philosopher Henry David Thoreau once said,

> *The greatest compliment that was ever paid me was when one asked me what I thought, and attended to my answer.*

2. Be comfortable with silence

When two old friends come together for a chat, or take a walk through the woods, you will notice that their conversation is frequently punctuated by bouts of silence. When there is silence, both remain relaxed and comfortable. When the conversation resumes, new ideas and perspectives emerge, thereby enriching their exchanges further. To conduct a meaningful conversation, we need to be mindful that occasional pauses are useful. In our frenzied world, we feel ill at ease when someone seems to have nothing to say. We quickly rush in to fill the gap.

In Eastern societies such as Japan, South Korea and China, silence is viewed as an integral part of conversation. When someone pauses, he may be gathering his thoughts before he articulates them. Or he may be a little unsure about whether he should speak up. This is frequently the case when someone is speaking with another person who occupies a higher position. The best stance we can take when there is silence is to stay calm and patient. And silent. Now is the opportunity to attend to the non-verbal cues that the other person is sending. Is he relaxed or tense? And his tone? Words convey informational content. But the emotional content is even more important.

According to Rachel Naomi Remen, a pioneer in the mind/body health movement, the greatest gift we can bring to another person is the silence in us. This is not the hostile silence that is filled with unspoken judgement and angry rejection. It is the silence of kindness, of rest and acceptance of people as they are. We all need this other silence. In its presence, we find refuge and strength to recover and grow. She also calls this *generous listening*.

3. Empathize

Author Stephen Covey[3] has a sound piece of advice for us all: *seek first to understand*. When we listen to understand, we put on the hat of a learner as opposed to an instructor's. A learner is curious. He does not have any preconceived notion about what he hopes to discover. He is open to what others are telling him, whatever it may be.

In contrast, we frequently behave like we know it all. We take it upon ourselves to validate what people say. We know what is correct. We pass judgement, if silently. A learner asks clarifying questions. Even as he probes, it is to find out more and not to make others wrong. He will not only increase his understanding; he may help the other parties look at the situation from another perspective.

4. Listen with the heart

Listening is a lost art. In the course of acquiring a formal education, growing up and working ourselves up the ranks, we have forgotten how to listen. This is a global phenomenon. When we seem to be listening to another person, countless thoughts are racing through our minds. We are fidgeting and our lips are ready to part. The moment the other person pauses, out comes our rejoinder at the speed of light. This is not listening. Neither is it a conversation. It is more like a tennis match between two archrivals, lobbing volleys at each other.

Thousands of years ago, people in ancient China discovered the secrets of real listening. Below is the character of the word *listening* in the traditional Chinese script. It is made up of the following pictograms: ears, eyes, heart and king.

Ears   Eyes

King   Heart

To be a good listener,[4] we must first recognize that the moment is NOW. The most important person is the person in our presence. He is the KING, so to speak. We will devote full attention to him by silencing all inner chatter and other activities. By engaging not only with our EARS and EYES but also our HEART, the true meaning of what is being said will become clear to us. Why is the heart involved? Shouldn't the ears and eyes be sufficient on their own? Perhaps not. What we hear and what we see may sometimes be inconsistent. For instance, people may appear to be agreeing and yet their body language and tone reveal reservation and discomfort. How do we reconcile between these two streams of conflicting signals? Our heart will tell us. According to 17th century French mathematician and physicist Blaise Pascal,

The heart has its reasons which reason knows not of.

5. Close the loop

When you listen deeply, you will discover insights that will surprise you. People whom you listen to know that they matter. When you come back again to listen to them and to share what you have done, they will be even more convinced that you are indeed empowering them.

When *deep listening* works hand in glove with *disruptive questioning*, we have pressed into service a dynamic duo. Chapter 10 explores the power of disruptive questioning.

CHAPTER 9

Part Three

PRACTICES

Q1: When you speak with someone, observe how you are listening when he speaks. Observe also how he listens when you speak. What are the differences in the listening ability between the two of you?

Q2: When was the last time you listened deeply? What surprised you? How can you make deep listening a habit?

DISRUPTIVE
QUESTIONING

... the important and difficult job is never to find the right answers, it is to find the right questions. For there are few things as useless — if not dangerous — as the right answer to the wrong question.

Peter Drucker (1909–2005)
American management consultant

Ngiam Tong Dow was one of Singapore's top policy makers. Once he told a story — probably apocryphal — regarding creativity. He was calling out a salient difference in the Chinese mindset towards learning compared with that of, say, the Jewish. When a Chinese boy goes home after school, his mother will be keen to find out how much knowledge her son has absorbed from his teachers. In contrast, a Jewish American mother will be more interested in knowing whether he has raised any interesting questions in class.

Culturally, people in Asia view learning as the acquisition of facts and knowledge. People in the West are amazed and even awed by how Asian parents produce so many maths whizzes and music prodigies. When Amy Chua's book *The Battle Hymn of the Tiger Mother* was released a few years ago, she said that it was supposed to be a story of how Chinese parents are better at raising kids than Western ones. Yet, when it comes to innovation and creativity, people in the West, especially the Americans, win hands-down.

Ironically, Asians such as the Chinese, Japanese and Koreans are weighed down by their learning and deference to authority. When confronted with a conundrum, they seek answers from what they already know. The Westerners, having no such baggage, are more free-spirited and adventurous. They ask questions to discover new possibilities. The father of modern physics, Albert Einstein, once said:

> *If I were given one hour to save the planet, I would spend 59 minutes defining the problem and one minute resolving it.*

Yet, what do we do when we are confronted with a thorny situation? Nearly all of us will define the problem hurriedly and then rush into looking for solutions. It is the *bias for action* mindset writ large. Like a frenzied oil prospector, we rush into drilling without even knowing the lay of the land.

Disruptive Questioning

What is the secret sauce of innovation? How do innovative people come up with breakthrough ideas while the rest of us stand in awe of them? Three business school professors[1] Jeff Dyer, Hal Gregersen and Clayton Christensen undertook a six-year study to uncover the origins of creative — and often disruptive — business strategies in particularly innovative companies. Altogether, they studied 25 innovative entrepreneurs and surveyed 3,000 executives and 500 individuals who had started innovative companies or invented new products. They were intrigued to learn that at the most creative companies, senior leaders don't delegate creative work. They get involved themselves personally. Their research shows such executives are familiar with five discovery skills:

1. Associating

2. Questioning

3. Observing

4. Experimenting

5. Networking

Together, these skills make up what they call the innovator's DNA. The professors have great news for leaders: the innovator's DNA can be cultivated.

In this chapter, I will focus on disruptive questioning. Let's start with an example of a consultant, Orit, who as a child growing up in Israel was fascinated by many things and always asking countless questions.

CHAPTER 10

Part Three

In the early 1980s, **ORIT** was fresh out of graduate school and new at consulting. Her first assignment was to help a steel manufacturer cut its cost to stay competitive. The client was a man in his 60s and did not welcome having women in the industry. According to him, women brought bad luck to any business! Unfazed, she pressed on and asked one question after another. At that time, there were two ways to make steel. The standard process was casting into individual ingots. Then there was a newfangled technology called continuous casting, where the molten steel was cast continuously and cut into slabs.

Orit's interest was piqued. Sensing its potential for the client, she visited Japan to study the continuous casting process firsthand. When she returned, she was convinced that this was a way for the client to turn its fortune around. But her suggestion fell on deaf ears. The executives and salespeople pushed back at her by saying that it wasn't technically feasible as they had 350 different products for customers. And how was continuous casting possible for so many different products when they had to add other materials simultaneously for each product? Orit wouldn't give up. She proceeded to visit customers and started asking them whether they really needed 350 products. And why? The initial response was invariably "yes, yes, and yes". She continued to probe deeper. She even went through each of the 350 products.

Armed with rich insights about why each product existed, Orit migrated from understanding *what was* to exploring *what might be*. She went on to explain that continuous casting offered cost advantages due to a unique feature: it allowed lower cost materials to be added during the process. She moved into disruptive territory by asking "what-if" questions that ignited the imagination of naysayers. Soon they were exploring possibilities such as:

- What if we are able to shrink the existing product line by 90 per cent?
- What if we cast continuously with a sharply reduced product line?
- What if we maximize the addition of cost-saving materials when casting the steel?

The executives realized that reducing the number of products was not only possible but was a profitable course of action. As other lower cost materials could be introduced while still meeting customers' specifications, this represented a breakthrough: raising productivity and efficiency while reducing cost significantly. Now convinced, the client built a new facility and quickly raced ahead of other US competitors.

CHAPTER 10

Part Three

This consultant is Orit Gadeish. Today, she is chairman of Bain & Company and is a world-renowned authority in the implementation of change within the corporation.

How to Ask Disruptive Questions

Innovators question conventional wisdom. They are always pushing the envelope and challenging assumptions. Not only do they ask many questions, there is a pattern as well. They take a two-stage approach: (1) Defining the lay of the land and then (2) Exploring the blue sky.

Defining the lay of the land

Like Einstein, innovative thinkers will hunker down to develop a deep understanding of the situation, before looking for solutions. At this stage, they will ask "what-is" questions followed by "why?" questions. It is useful to remind ourselves that we will get richer responses if we ask open-ended as opposed to closed-ended questions. For instance, a typical "what-is" question is "What is the purpose of this feature in the product?" This is an open-ended question. This is an invitation for the other party to speak his mind freely. The results will be an unconstrained flow of ideas. If you had asked, "Are you sure you need this feature?" this will be a closed-ended question. It would put him on the defensive and might lead him down the path of justifying its existence.

To get the most out of a conversation, consider using the dynamic duo of deep listening and disruptive questioning. Let's refer to Orit Gadeish's project with the steel manufacturer to illustrate how she could have defined the lay of the land. The "what-is" questions could have been:

- What is the current process in the plant?
- How many products are you making?
- What is peculiar about each product?
- Where are the bottlenecks?

The "why?" questions may be:

- Why cast in ingots?
- Why not adopt the continuous casting process?
- What are the pros and cons for the two different processes?

We may take guidance from the five-whys questioning technique pioneered by Taiichi Ohno, the architect of the famed Toyota Production System:

CHAPTER 10

Part Three

Observe ... Without preconception and with a blank mind, repeat "why" five times to every matter.

By asking "why" at least five times, we will get to understand the resistance to continuous casting. Frequently, to everybody's surprise, there may not even be a real concrete reason. It usually boils down to unchallenged assumptions, fear and lack of understanding or just sheer inertia.

Exploring the blue sky

Blue-sky questions are meant to illuminate and inspire. They invite your dialogue partner to take a flight of fancy and set aside worldly constraints for a while and fantasize. Studies have shown that down-to-earth, delivery-minded managers — the custodians — do not spend time asking blue-sky questions. Why so? According to Neil Postman and Charles Weingartner, early advocates of inquiry-based living and learning, it is because they aren't willing to look stupid and be viewed as uncooperative and disagreeable. And, I might add, in Asia, they don't want to lose face. Neither do they want others to lose face.

In contrast, creative managers ask them regularly. They usually start with "what-if" questions. Again referring to the steel-making case, these are some questions that will spur creative taking:

- What if demand goes through the roof?
- What if your customers prefer the continuous casting process?
- What if the Japanese enter your market?

Dyer, Gregersen and Christensen[2] have a paradoxical recommendation that will raise creative provocation to another level. We

tend to think constraints stifle and even suffocate us. They see it differently. Just as we know intuitively that necessity is the mother of all inventions, they believe constraints will bring out the iconoclast in us. Ask "what-if" questions to impose constraints:

- What if customers ask for 40 per cent reduction in cost?
- What if the factory space has been halved?

In India, there is a concept called *jugaad* or *frugal innovation*.[3] Instead of *the bigger is better approach* that huge multinationals in the West are used to, the Indians are going the opposite direction: doing more with less or innovating frugally through improvisation, ingenuity and cleverness. An example is an inexpensive clay mini-fridge that doesn't use electricity to keep perishable foods cool. It was created by a rural entrepreneur for Indian villages where electricity may not always be reliable. Many start-ups in China, Brazil, and throughout Africa and Europe are embracing *jugaad* principles as well. Finally, we may ask "what-if" questions to eliminate constraints:

- What if we have no budgetary constraint?
- What if customers clamour for continuous casting?

Appreciative Inquiry[4]

How can leaders engender a climate of curiosity and creativity? This can be done through a form of questioning known as appreciative inquiry (AI). Let's now examine a case involving two managers in the same organization. Both faced similar challenges. However, the approaches adopted were quite different.

CHAPTER 10

Part Three

After graduating from the same university, **PETER** and **JOHN** joined the same well-known software design company in San Jose. Both were smart, ambitious and hard-working. Peter was very intense, while John was more relaxed and friendly. They were assigned to work in different projects. Within 24 months, both had become programme leaders. There were a lot of challenges involving technical issues, delays, frequently changing customer specifications, budget constraints and strong personalities.

Peter and John had two diametrically opposed ways of handling challenges. To Peter, problems were symptoms of incompetence and oversight. Someone had screwed up. And that person had to be called to account. However, John saw a silver lining behind every storm cloud. Although he was just as anxious about delays and other slip-ups, he chose to treat each situation as a chance to learn together and get better. He had a rather unique philosophy about working with people. He said this to me: "I learn from playing basketball that players who are able to stay calm and have fun while under pressure will perform at a higher level than those who get flustered and lose their nerves. Stormy weather and curved ball are opportunities to dig deep within ourselves to find resources that we may never know existed when the sun is shining!"

CHAPTER 10

Part Three

In many organizations, when issues are encountered the default reaction is to take a problem-focused approach. If leaders take this too far, they will create a fear culture. Nobody wants to speak up as they know they will be blamed. This was the climate that

Peter created. Contrast this with the solution-focused approach adopted by John. Team members see a world of possibilities despite setbacks. They go forward with optimism and renewed resolve every day.

How to Adopt AI in Organizations

Instead of focusing on what is not working, AI reverses the traditional problem-focused approach into a solution-focused approach. Here are four steps to follow:

1. *Focus on the positive.* For instance, a solution-focused question to improve customer satisfaction is, "When customers are pleased with our service, what do they tell us?" A problem-focused question to avoid initially is "What upset our customers?"

2. *Leverage your strengths.* Do more of what the organization is already very good at. This stirs the imagination of people. It will spur them to want to excel, because they already know it is working very well.

3. *Look for common themes in successes.* Encourage people to share stories of what they have done well in. Identify common themes. Weave them into a set of shared images for the future.

4. *Create the new future together.* The final step is to tap into the collective energy and creativity of the workforce by engaging them to create a sense of shared purpose and vision for the future.

A caveat is in order. Leaders must guard against coming across as the eternal optimist, no matter what. There will be good and bad times. Occasionally, someone has fouled up badly due to personal negligence. At other times, complacency may have set in. On such occasions, taking the problem-focused approach will serve as a wake-up call. For instance, if one particular aspect of service continues to irk clients, then it is time to ask: "Why is this problem still not fixed? Whose responsibility is this?"

Team members who are giving their all will be watching. They expect parties who aren't pulling their weight to be held accountable. Leaders must not flinch from doing the necessary. When performance standards are enforced, everyone feels uplifted. Good people appreciate bosses who are tough and fair. And now, onwards to addressing complexity in the next chapter.

PRACTICES

Q1: Observe how discussions are conducted in your company. Using three to five different words, how will you describe the climate? How do participants feel as they end the meeting? Is it a problem-focused or solution-focused approach?

Q2: What steps can you take to ignite creativity in your company?

CHAPTER 10

Part Three

COMPLEXITY

Let us try for once not to be right.

Tristan Tzara (1896–1963)
Romanian and French poet, essayist and
performance artist

M anaging organizations today is fundamentally different from a generation ago. The biggest factor is the level of complexity that people have to cope with. Leaders have to constantly grapple with the daunting task of making sense of what is happening. And it is getting harder to do so. Admittedly, every generation has the same thing to say about the era that they are in. Complex situations have always existed, of course. Business and life are always full of surprises and constant changes.

Towards the latter part of the 20th century, the revolutionary impact of the Internet led to a transformation of commerce and communication. Suddenly, information and knowledge became instantly accessible in every part of the world. The democratization of news and information hastened the globalization of businesses. In today's context, social media tools such as Facebook, Twitter, WhatsApp, LinkedIn, Instagram, etc., have resulted in a hyper-connected world. Systems that used to be separate now have a high degree of interconnectedness and interdependence. Because the interactions occur in unexpected ways, it is harder to make sense of things. Herein lies the complexity. This impacts almost everything that we come in contact with every day: the issues we tackle, the services we provide, the products we design and market, the work that we do and the people we intermingle with.

A complex situation is much more difficult to handle than a merely complicated one. We need to know the difference. If we mix the two up, and try to handle a complex situation as though it is a complicated one, there will be adverse ramifications.

Simple to Complicated to Complex

Let's start with simple systems. There are few interactions and are characterized by clear cause-and-effect relationships that are easy to understand. For instance, filing income tax returns through the Internet. The steps are easy to follow and if there are problems, they can be identified and remedied readily. Complicated systems have many moving parts. Though there is a clear relationship between cause and effect, it is not visible to everybody. There may be multiple right answers. Zeroing in on the preferred ones requires domain expertise. Repairing a computer that has malfunctioned involves a series of complicated but predictable steps. But when carried

CHAPTER 11

Part Three

out by a well-trained technician, the computer will be back to working order in a short while. In a complicated system, at least one right answer exists.

However, in a complex situation, the right answers are far from obvious. There are many heterogeneous agents that interact with each other. And because they interact in unexpected and ever-changing ways, it is harder to predict the outcome. In a real way, the whole becomes greater than the sum of the parts. In a recent *Harvard Business Review* article[1] by Gokce Sargut and Rita Gunther McGrath, these distinctions are offered:

> Practically speaking, the main difference between complicated and complex systems is that with the former, one can predict outcomes knowing the starting conditions. In a complex system, the same starting conditions can produce different outcomes, depending on the interactions of the elements in the system.

For example, building a state-of-the-art hospital to serve a metropolis is a complicated project, but trying to contain the spread of a contagious disease is a complex problem. Building a sophisticated highway system is complicated, but tackling massive traffic congestion is a complex situation.

David Horth[2] and Charles Paulus from the Center for Creative Leadership, headquartered in Greensboro, define complex challenges as follows:

> Complex challenges are situations or contexts that defy existing approaches or solutions. They are central in importance and demand decisive action. Yet, because the organization, team, or individual does not know how to act, there is also a need to slow down and reflect.

You know you are facing a complex challenge if:

- You are feeling stuck and getting frustrated. Earlier attempts to tackle the problems have not succeeded.
- You have called in the experts for help. Yet, you are now realizing that domain expertise may not be the solution. Even the experts are baffled.
- The people involved disagree about the nature of the challenge and what should be done.

There are differing views on assumptions and root causes. To grapple with complexity, we need a new mental model. Complexity does not lend itself to tidy mathematical and linear analysis. Hans Peter Durr, formerly of the Max Planck Institute, said:

> ... it does not help to analyze things in more detail. The more specific the information, the less relevant it is.

Complexity researchers say our analytical tools have not kept up. Instead of focusing on separate parts of the challenge, we need to understand the whole system with the interconnecting networks within. An ancient Sufi teaching cited in the Introduction of this book captures this shift in focus:

> You think because you understand "one" you must also understand "two", because one and one make two. But you must also understand "and".

According to organizational behaviourist Margaret Wheatley, such a manner of thinking is difficult for the Western mind to grasp. In fact, many readers of the early draft of this book told me they were perplexed by the Sufi quote. Yet those familiar with

CHAPTER 11

Part Three

Buddhist beliefs understand this intuitively. Respected Zen master Thích Nhất Hạnh[3] explains:

> *All things depend on all others for their existence …*
> *All beings rely on the law of dependent co-rising.*
> *The source of one thing is all things.*

Leading a Large-Scale Change Programme

About a year and a half ago, a new **CEO** was appointed to helm a large government agency in a Southeast Asian country. He was a high-flying military leader. This new role was a transition for him into the public sector in preparation for a political career. A key deliverable was to transform the agency that over the years had become inwardly focused and unresponsive to external changes. In the first few months, he spoke quite extensively to various stakeholders and senior people in the agency. Once he had "sufficient" information and understanding, he initiated a large-scale change programme to simplify the structure and processes. His intention was good. It was to streamline the organization to create a more agile, collaborative and responsive agency.

Ten task forces were created to focus on areas that needed attention. The senior managers were supportive and enthusiastic. As the various teams pushed ahead with their work, it soon became clear no task force could fulfil all its objectives without involving other task forces. And as the degree of interconnectedness became apparent, a sense of anxiety and fear crept in. The boundaries that were defined for each task force initially gave a sense of certainty and control. But now they were beginning to feel trapped and boxed in. The divisions and departments had been used to working in silos for more than two decades. Reaching out and learning to work with each other in a give-and-take fashion was a totally alien concept.

It didn't help that the new CEO wasn't a great listener. He was quite above it all and autocratic in his approach. He repeatedly emphasized that it was up to all the task forces to work out with each other what was best for the agency. Fatigue and frustration began to creep in visibly. Rumours began swirling around about new functions to be created, redundant functions to be eliminated and people to be moved around. Soon task force leaders began to act in strange ways as observed by subordinates. They became overly cautious and started to take their eyes off the running of the day-to-day operations. Many people could no longer cope and opted for early retirement. Those who remained were completely disillusioned. They just wanted to move on and implement something or anything, so that they could get on with their lives. Others decided to sit this out, as received wisdom was that "top leaders come and go every three years, and this too shall pass".

Part Three CHAPTER 11

The example just discussed is real. What we have seen is the typical approach that leaders adopt when they are faced with leading large-scale change, i.e. they treat it as though it is a complicated machinery which has malfunctioned and needs to be overhauled. The impact of this linear approach is that additional complicatedness

is layered onto an already complex situation. This comes in the form of revised procedures and processes, interface structures, shifting centres of power, and redefined roles and responsibilities. In the frenzy of bringing greater clarity and alignment within each system, people forget about the interconnection and interdependence between various systems. The net result: greater confusion, frustration and fragmentation.

Thirty years of research by retired Harvard Business School professor and leadership/change expert John Kotter[4] have proven that 70 per cent of all major change efforts in organizations fail. Why? Because organizations often do not take the holistic approach required to see the change through.

Kotter first introduced his legendary eight-stage change process in 1994. This became an instant hit for organizations seeking a methodology to lead change. Now decades later in the midst of constant turbulence and disruption, he recommends a revised approach for corporations: adopt a dual operating system.

In essence, let the traditional hierarchies and managerial processes remain. This is the organization's first operating system, which will continue to run the enterprise. Then in parallel, set up a second operating system to identify important hazards quickly, formulate creative strategic solutions nimbly and implement them speedily.

The second operating system is built on a fluid, network-like structure to continually formulate and implement strategy. It will be staffed by volunteers and will be free of bureaucratic encumbrances, permitting a level of individualism, creativity and innovation that will elude the first operating system.

Leaders who are parachuted into underperforming companies are naturally anxious to make their mark at one fell swoop. Before

CHAPTER 11

Part Three

acting, they should take heed of the wise words of mathematician and philosopher Alfred North Whitehead: "Every leader, to be effective, must simultaneously adhere to the symbols of change and revision and the symbols of tradition and stability." If Carly Fiorina had contemplated Whitehead's advice, her tenure as CEO of Hewlett-Packard would have been a happier one.

Shall We Turn to the Experts?

What then is a more helpful way to think about complexity? Should we, as we have done so in the past, run to the experts for help? It is natural for us to defer to experts. Good leaders will surround themselves with the smartest specialists so that they can avail themselves of their deepest insights. Unfortunately, the best experts may not have the solutions that we seek. This is the surprising conclusion of a two-decade study by psychologist Philip Tetlock[5] begun in 1984. Today, he is a professor at the University of Pennsylvania. He picked nearly 300 experts whose job was to comment or advise on political and economic trends. These were intellectual heavyweights: political scientists, economists, lawyers and diplomats. Tetlock asked them to make specific, quantifiable forecasts — 82,000 predictions in all — and then waited to see whether their forecast came true. The results? The predictions of these experts were only a little bit better than random guesses. Tetlock wrote:

> It made virtually no difference whether the participants had doctorates, whether they were economists, political scientists, journalists, or historians, whether they had policy experience or access to classified information, or whether they had logged many or few years of experience.

Tetlock also found that specialists are not significantly more reliable than non-specialists. In one study, data from a test used to diagnose brain damage were given to a group of clinical psychologists and their secretaries. The psychologists' diagnoses were no better than the secretaries'.

Why do experts perform below expectations? Why is it knowing a lot can actually make a person less reliable as a forecaster? To explain this, Tetlock borrowed a metaphor from a famous essay by Isaiah Berlin[6] entitled *The Hedgehog and the Fox*. In it, Berlin quoted the Greek poet Archilochus:

> *The fox knows many things, but the hedgehog knows one big thing.*

Tetlock explains that low-scoring experts are like hedgehogs. These are narrow specialists who know one big thing. They tend to extrapolate that one big thing into new domains. When questioned, they get impatient with those who do not get it. Their confidence in their ability to forecast is considerable.

To Tetlock, high-scorers behave like foxes. These are thinkers who know many small things in their discipline. Though highly competent and credible, they stay grounded and are wary of grand schemes. They are open and flexible in evaluating disparate events and diverse data before synthesizing them into a coherent picture. They remain rather diffident about their own forecasting prowess.

In an opinion piece entitled *Learning How to Think* published in *The New York Times* in March 2009, Nicholas D. Kristof[7] weighed in on this interesting paradox. As he puts it,

CHAPTER 11

Part Three

There's evidence that what matters in making a sound forecast or decision isn't so much knowledge or expertise as good judgement, or, to be more precise, the way a person's mind thinks.

He described an example of the awe that an expert inspires in all of us. This is the *Dr Fox effect*. It is named after a series of psychology experiments in which an actor was paid to give a meaningless presentation to professional educators. The actor was introduced to the audience as Dr Myron L. Fox, an imaginary character, and described as an eminent authority on the application of mathematics to human behaviour. He then proceeded to give a lecture about a mathematics games theory as applied to physical education. Though it was well delivered with jokes and interesting neologisms, it was by design pointless and devoid of substance. Afterwards, the participants were asked to rate Dr Fox. Most people were impressed. "Excellent presentation, enjoyed listening", wrote one. Another protested: "Too intellectual a presentation."

The Adaptive Organization

In tackling increasingly complex challenges, leaders will need to take the whole-brained approach. We covered this in Chapter 7. The first set of skills resides in our left hemisphere. They are our trusty logical, analytical and results-oriented capabilities. Excellence in these is typically what people are hired and rewarded for. But in and by themselves these aren't sufficient. The second set is less familiar to us. They are related to the right hemisphere and enable us to be more intuitive, playful, curious, conceptual, synthesizing and artistic.

CHAPTER 11

Part Three

Far ahead of his time, Lao Zi offered us a preeminently practical principle in life: *Less is sometimes more.* The Chinese have a phrase for this — *wei wu wei* — which literally means "doing not doing", or learning to trust yourself. In his words:[8]

> A wise traveler adapts his plans
> according to the terrain.
> A good dancer silences his thoughts and
> goes with the music
> An astute leader considers the data
> and trusts his instincts.

How then do we address complex challenges? Stuart Kauffmann[9] and John Holland, complexity theorists affiliated with the multidisciplinary Santa Fe Institute recommend that we adopt the evolutionary approach. This means we should mimic nature through mutation and selection. Instead of engaging in an exhaustive and time-consuming search for the *best* solution, it is far better to look for a variety of possible solutions, implement what *works for now*, and then continuing to adapt through trial and error. There are four key steps we may consider in this adaptive and experimental approach.[10]

1. Explore

This is the first and most important step. As with most things in organizational settings, the leader has to set the tone here. System thinker Margaret J. Wheatley defines the challenge clearly when she says the leader has to shift from hero to host. The take-charge autocratic CEO we encountered in the earlier example is the antithesis of a *host*.

Part Three | CHAPTER 11

A host willingly and sincerely puts his ego aside. He acknowledges that he needs his colleagues as full contributors. He values their skills and insights. He then proceeds to harvest fresh insights through meaningful conversations among people from many parts of the systems. But Wheatley cautions against letting it become a talkfest that goes on and on with no end in sight. Hosting leaders must do the following:[11]

- Provide conditions and group processes for people to work together.
- Make available resources of time, the scarcest commodity of all.
- Insist that people and the system learn from experience, frequently.
- Offer unequivocal support — people know the leader is there for them.
- Keep the bureaucracy at bay, creating oases (or bunkers) where people are less encumbered by senseless demands for reports and administrivia.
- Play defence with other leaders who want to take back control, who are critical that people have been given too much freedom.
- Reflect back to people on a regular basis how they are doing, what they are accomplishing, how far they have journeyed, etc.
- Work with people to develop relevant measures of progress to make their achievements visible.
- Value conviviality and esprit de corps — not false rah-rah activities, but the spirit that arises in any group that accomplishes difficult work together.

CHAPTER 11

Part Three

2. Boundary span

A Center for Creative Leadership study[12] emphasizes the power of boundary spanning. While boundaries create borders that divide people, boundaries are also frontiers. Hence, organizations need to boundary span to create direction, alignment and commitment across five types of boundaries:

1. *Vertical:* Rank, class, seniority, authority, power

2. *Horizontal:* Expertise, function, peers

3. *Stakeholders:* Partners, constituencies, value chain, communities

4. *Demographic:* Gender, generation, nationality, culture, personality, ideology

5. *Geographic:* Location, region, market distance

When leaders and groups effectively span boundaries, they tap into and leverage unique capabilities that reside in various parts of the organizations, forge common ground and discover new frontiers.

3. Experiment

Pick a few promising ideas and try them out. Try them out in a context where failure is survivable. This is a tough step, to put it mildly. In many *high-performing organizations* the F word is taboo. Many people who are labelled *high fliers* carry a heavy burden on their shoulders. It is their organization's way of saying,

> *"I know you are the best. You know it too.
> So don't you go and mess things up!"*

CHAPTER 11

Part Three

Their instinctive response is to play safe too. Take no risks. Stay in the comfort zone. Hold on to the wins you have amassed so far. Don't play to win. Play not to lose. No wonder organizations populated by the so-called best and brightest are mired in mediocrity.[13]

Yet, how do we stumble upon a lucky break unless we try out many new things and fail frequently? We need a culture where failure is permissible. By failing frequently and learning from each failure, we are moving closer and closer to the solutions we seek. We either learn to fail or fail to learn.

4. Adapt

The process of experimenting can be nerve-wracking as well as liberating. It can also go on endlessly. At a certain point, it is time for action. Experimenters need to have the gumption to move into implementation.

Success is still not in the bag. Failure may still raise its ugly head. When we come up short, we will need to pause and recollect our thoughts. What have we learnt? How can we do it better? This is when resilience will be needed. When dealing with complex challenges, one never knows for sure whether we will succeed. But if we don't adapt again and again, our demise is certain.

CHAPTER 11

Part Three

PRACTICES

Q1: When in doubt, have you ever said, "I don't know"? When should you say this? When should you not say this?

Q2: Are you a fox or a hedgehog? In tackling complex situations, what is your preferred course of action?

Q3: We discussed the differences between technical and adaptive challenges in Chapter 6. We also mentioned the metaphors about organizations in the Introduction of this book: machine *versus* the living system. What dominant thinking influenced the CEO when he mandated the large-scale change? How will you do it now if you are in his shoes?

Q4: Observe the talented people in your organization. Do they play to win? Or do they play not to lose?

PART FOUR
LEADING WISELY

*By three methods we may learn wisdom. First, by reflection,
which is noblest; second, by imitation, which is easiest;
and third, by experience, which is the bitterest.*

Confucius (551–479 BC)
Chinese philosopher

Chapter 12

REFLECTION

Life can only be understood backwards,
but it must be lived forwards.

Søren Kierkegaard (1813–1855)
Danish philosopher

A question that has always fascinated me for the longest time is why some leaders gain more from their experiences than others. We see this all the time in our own lives. People with broadly similar backgrounds graduated from the same school and went out into the world at the same time. They joined different organizations and performed different roles. Then 30 years later, they meet for a class reunion. What will they observe of the changes in each other? Here are some possible snapshots:

1. Not all who were star students, or athletes or champion debaters, will have excelled in their chosen fields. In contrast, the more nondescript may have made more of their humbler attributes.

2. The journey through life will have left its imprint on each person differently. For some, not that much has changed apart from the greying hair, the undeniable wrinkles and the greater bulk around the waist. Some have become more introspective, quieter or more subdued. But for a small minority, life has been transformative. They have become visibly different personalities from what they were decades back.

3. Now in their late 50s, most are planning to retire or transition into the autumn of their lives. But there are a few who are still brimming with ideas and moving into their second or third career.

This is a timeless question, and not a simple one to answer. It is part of the great debate about whether leaders are born or bred. Increasingly though, there is evidence that how one develops and grows as a leader is dependent on his ability to find meaning in negative events and learn from the most trying circumstances. In short, have we become the authors of our lives? Or have we lived a life based on the script written by our culture, tradition or some figures of authority lurking in our psyche?

Observations from a 20th Century Novelist

In the 1930s, William Somerset Maugham — a British novelist, playwright and short-story writer — was a highly regarded author. He graduated in 1897 from St. Thomas's Hospital Medical School in London and qualified as a doctor, but abandoned medicine after the success of his novels and plays. Maugham travelled widely and many of his stories were about his experiences in China. In his collection, there is a short story entitled *The Rolling Stone*[1] that speaks about how one's experience could be unrivalled and yet one could remain untouched.

I heard his extraordinary story before I saw him and I expected someone of striking appearance. It seemed to me that anyone who had gone through such singular experiences must have in his outer man something singular too. But I found a person in whose aspect there was nothing remarkable. He was smaller than the average, somewhat frail, sunburned, with hair beginning to turn grey though he was under thirty, and brown eyes. He looked like anyone else, and you might see him half a dozen times before remembering who he was. If you had happened upon him behind the counter of a department store or on a stool in a broker's office you would have thought him perfectly in place. But you would have noticed him as little as you noticed the counter or the stool. There was so little in him to attract attention that in the end it became intriguing: his face, empty of significance, reminded you of the blank wall of a Manchu palace, in a sordid street, behind which you knew were painted courtyards, carved dragons, and heaven knows what subtle intricacy of life.

For his whole career was remarkable. The son of a veterinary surgeon, he had been a reporter in the London police courts and then had gone as steward on board a merchant ship to Buenos Aires. There he had deserted and somehow or other had worked his way across South America. From a port in Chile he managed to get to the Marquesas, where for six months he had lived on the natives always ready to offer hospitality to a white man, and then, begging a passage on a schooner to Tahiti had shipped to Amoy as second mate of an old tub which carried Chinese labour to the Society Islands.

That was nine years before I met him and since then he had lived in China. First he got work with the B.A.T. Company, but after a couple of years he found it monotonous; and having acquired knowledge of the language he entered the employment of a firm which distributed patent medicines through the length and breadth of the land. For three years he wandered in province after province, selling pills, and at the end of it had saved eight hundred dollars. He cut himself adrift once more.

He began the most remarkable of his adventures. He set out from Peking on a journey right across the country, traveling in the guise of a poor Chinaman, with his roll of bedding, his Chinese pipe, and his tooth-brush. He stayed in the Chinese inns, sleeping on the kangs huddled up with fellow-wayfarers, and ate the Chinese food. This alone is no mean feat. He used the train but little, going for the most part on foot, by cart, or by river. He went through Shensi and Shansi; he walked on the windy plateaus of Mongolia and risked his life in barbaric Turkestan; he spent long weeks with nomads of the desert and traveled with the caravans that carried the brick tea across the arid wilderness of Gobi. At last, four years later, having spent his last dollar, he reached Peking once more.

He set looking for a job. The easiest way to earn money seemed to write, and the editor of the English papers in China offered to take a series of articles on his journey. I suppose his only difficulty was to choose from the fullness of his experience. He knew much which he was perhaps the only Englishman to know. He had seen all manner of things, quaint, impressive, terrible, amusing, and unexpected. He wrote twenty-four articles, I will not say that they were unreadable, for they showed a careful and a sympathetic observation; but he had seen everything at haphazard, as it were, and they were but the material of art. They were like the catalogue of the Army and Navy Stores, a mine to the imaginative man, but the foundation of literature rather than literature itself. He was the field naturalist who patiently collects infinity of facts, but has no gift for generalization: they remain facts that await the synthesis of minds more complicated than his. He collected neither plants nor beasts, but men. His collection was unrivalled, but his knowledge of it slender.

When I met him I sought to discern how the variety of his experience had affected him; but though he was full of anecdote, a jovial, friendly creature, willing to talk at length of all he had seen, I could not discover that any of his adventures had intimately touched him. The instinct to do all the queer things he had done showed that there was in him a streak of queerness. The civilized work irked him and he had a passion to get away from the beaten trail. The oddities of life amused him. He had an insatiable curiosity. But I think his experiences were merely of the body and were never translated into experiences of the soul. Perhaps that is why at the bottom you felt he was commonplace. The insignificance of his mien was a true index to the insignificance of his soul. Behind the blank wall was blankness.

> That was certainly why with so much to write about he wrote tediously, for in writing the important thing is less richness of material than richness of personality.

Learning from Extraordinary People

In the late 20th century, Howard Gardner[2] spent more than ten years deeply immersed in a study of the lives of extraordinary individuals. In his pursuit of what he calls the genus *mind extraordinaire*, the exceptional people he selected were drawn from a wide range of human experiences. They included Martha Graham and Pablo Picasso, Wolfgang Mozart and Igor Stravinsky, Mao Zedong and Franklin Roosevelt, Virginia Woolf and Margaret Mead as well as Mahatma Gandhi and Sigmund Freud. In his book *Extraordinary Minds*, Gardner raises some interesting questions:

- What lessons can we ordinary people learn from the study of these remarkable individuals?
- What might promote a greater degree of creativity or excellence in our contemporary world?
- How might we increase the likelihood that human excellence be mobilized for the common good?

Gardner's synthesis suggests that it is not *raw powers* that distinguish the extraordinary. Rather, there are three recurring characteristics:

- An ability to *reflect* — often explicitly — on the events of their lives, large as well as small.
- A knack for identifying and *leveraging* their own strengths.

- The ability to bounce back from defeats and *frame* the setbacks as learning opportunities.

For the rest of this chapter, we will talk about reflecting and framing. We have covered leveraging your strengths in Part 1 of the book.

Reflecting

The world we live in seems designed to thwart serious reflection. Most people lead an overworked, hectic and jam-packed existence. Finding time to reflect regularly is uncommon. During the day, we engage in myriad actions and reactions. Then at the end of it, we are so worn out that we are grateful to spend a little time with the family, have dinner, chill out a little and get some sleep. Soon a new day beckons and we are back to the merry-go-round.

I have also met many senior managers who have said that apart from not being able to find the time, they do not know how to go about reflecting. Why reflect? These are the key reasons:

- Harness the lessons from our experience.
- Discover newer, different perspectives and more possibilities.
- Achieve greater depth and insights.
- It is a distinctive way of working.

Harness the lessons from our experience

Someone once said that life is what happens to us when we are too busy doing something else. Nearly ten years ago, I was working at home when I noticed that the room was getting stuffy. A quick check showed that the air-conditioning unit was in need of a clean-up. Removing the filters and washing them was the easy

CHAPTER 12

Part Four

part. Then I decided to do a more thorough job that involved scrubbing out the grime from the cooling fins.

In my haste to complete this rather odious chore so that I could get on with my real work, I literally ripped out the plastic cover without removing the screws. It was a tad too late when I realized what I had done. The two corners where the screws had been attached were broken off. Later, I had to spend many frustrating minutes clumsily contorting some wire hooks to secure the cover back onto the air-conditioner.

Today, the trusty old faithful continues to purr away delivering cool air. The hooks are still there — an embarrassing reminder of the maxim: measure twice, cut once. Every once in a while when I chomp at the bit, my wife and two daughters will remind me about the *air-con thing*.

The *air-con thing* is an allegory for various mishaps that we may encounter in our daily lives. My learning from this mundane incident is that when we are anxious, our focus narrows. We zero in quickly onto what we think is the best approach and ignore other possibilities. Then wham, we execute.

With a little bit of luck, we may come up smiling. More frequently than not, we will have instead an "Oh sh*t!" moment. It is a trifle late. There may be unintended consequences. An "Oh sh*t!" moment may be a chance to learn something useful, but only if we consciously pause and reflect. Accumulatively, the lessons learnt will help us navigate through work and life with greater wisdom.

Discover newer, different perspectives and more possibilities

When we reflect, we are having a deep and quiet conversation with ourselves. We are turning over the events of the day in our minds and letting our inner voice speak to us. By staying calm and allowing our thoughts to range unfettered, we give expression to repressed ideas and ill-defined scraps of our imagination buried in our subconscious.

Provocative questions may suddenly pop up. Something that someone said which we had dismissed returns with a certain alienated majesty. An idea completely unconnected to the topic in hand suddenly barges in. When seemingly disparate thoughts from different spaces start to fall into place, we experience a sudden awakening.

Achieve greater depth and insights[3]

In organizational settings, many managers have lost the ability to think deeply and extract meaningful insights beyond the obvious. The most frequently cited excuse is not enough time. True, having sufficient time for deep thinking is necessary. But the real culprit is a combination of factors that characterize the organization's corporate climate. They consist of:

- A desire to produce quick, short-term results.
- The fear of challenging the status quo and mainstream ideas from the powers-that-be.
- A lack of managerial support for risk-taking.
- The reluctance, or indeed inability, to deep-dive into the data presented.

In one company, senior leaders offered to make special arrangements for a select group of managers so that they had more time to think about important issues. Astonishingly, not one person opted to participate. This is not at all uncommon. Deep reflection and thinking is hard work. It is also scary. It involves challenging assumptions. Perhaps, for far too long we have been tiptoeing around certain sacred cows. Dare we suggest that they be slaughtered now?

Corporations generally don't do a good job in encouraging deep reflection. So it is really up to the individuals themselves. Those who are willing to go down this less trodden path will add a real competitive advantage to their companies. They will see the missing connections between dots. Although others may have the same information, they will not see the link until it is explicitly pointed out.

It is a distinctive way of working

Reflection is not a retreat from work.[4] While some leaders may be able to withdraw temporarily, most recognize that the tough issues that they face must be answered by staying on the job. Marcus Aurelius, the Roman emperor and philosopher who ruled a vast expanse of Europe, North Africa and the Middle East from AD 161 to AD 180, was certainly a busy and heavily burdened executive. Yet, he was able to maintain calmness in the midst of exacting business. During the last years of his life, he kept a record of his reflections, observations and self-criticism. His personal journal is now known as *Meditations*.[5] He was writing for himself and not for anyone else. Nonetheless, the record of his rumination is his gift to posterity.

Aurelius advised himself that nowhere can a man find a quieter or more untroubled retreat than in his own soul. Busy leaders must recognize the danger of rushing to judgement of complicated issues. When we are at the coalface, we lose a sense of perspective. And that is when we must get on the balcony, see the larger patterns and then return to the thick of action with greater clarity. Sound

CHAPTER 12

Part Four

reflection is not a matter of time out; it involves the quality of time in. Hence, for effective leaders, it is actually a distinctive way of working.

Framing

Something disappointing has occurred. The project did not take off as planned. There is a lot of frustration felt by everybody. What will the bosses say? This is the proverbial glass-half-empty versus glass-half-full mindset. How do you react habitually?

Framing is the ability to construe experiences in such a way that we can draw apt lessons from them, stay positive and energized, and get on with our work with renewed resolve. This goes hand-in-hand with the habit of reflection. Committing to excelling in our chosen field is not going to be a smooth journey. There will be ups and downs, frequently more downs than ups.

Truth be told, we learn more from setbacks than successes. The most traumatic experiences have the potential to make or break us. Warren Bennis[6] calls such experiences *crucibles,* after the vessels mediaeval alchemists used in their attempts to turn base metals into gold. In his extensive study of outstanding leaders, he discovered that the crucible experiences that they had undergone were trials and tests that forced them into deep reflection to question who they were and what mattered to them. Through the examination of their values and assumptions, these leaders honed their judgement and they emerged from the crucible stronger and surer of themselves, with their sense of purpose changed in some fundamental way.

How an Asian Leader Found His Voice

It was the quarterly business review for top leaders of an American multinational in New Jersey. Takada san was the general manager of the subsidiary in Japan. He had recently succeeded the previous GM, an American, and was attending the global review for the first time. Though his business had achieved excellent results, he was visibly nervous.

This was the midpoint of Day 3. Takada san had just presented his business results in the morning. The participants were all hungry and were filing out of the conference room to head for lunch. Ahead of Takada san were two American executives whom he had not met so far. The two of them were chatting.

> **Person 1:** Do you know that Asian gentleman — Takada san — I think his name is?
>
> **Person 2:** Nope, we have not spoken to each other yet. He's rather quiet. Maybe, I'll talk to him during cocktail this evening. Why do you ask?
>
> **Person 1:** It just seems a little strange. He says very little. The conference ends this evening. Yet apart from his short business review this morning, we have heard nothing else from him. Does he have any opinions at all?
>
> **Person 2:** You're right. Maybe he's shy. But then what's the point of coming all the way from Japan if he has nothing to contribute?

Takada san was quite disturbed and embarrassed by what he had overheard. On the long flight back to Tokyo, he had a lot of time to reflect. He realized that it was true that he had said little throughout the conference. He knew the reasons:

- Like nearly all Japanese, Takada san was uncomfortable about "showing off" at meetings. In Japan, as in most Asian cultures, there is a saying that the nail which stands out gets hammered down.
- If he had spoken up, perhaps, his views might not be that useful or original. Why waste the time of other participants?
- What if others disagreed with what he said? Wouldn't that lead to loss of face?

The weight of centuries of Japanese culture and tradition was bearing down on Takada san. Speaking up and claiming more air time just didn't seem right. Yet he knew his Western colleagues didn't view his reticence with a lot of empathy. They expected him to contribute his views!

In the weeks ahead, he chatted with many Asians, especially Japanese friends, who were stationed in the United States. He wanted to know whether they had similar struggles. Gradually, he reframed his perspective as follows:

- Participants at meetings are there for a purpose. They should share their views openly because meetings become more productive when everybody contributes. Speaking up is an expectation, and is not showing off.
- There is no need to stress oneself out by insisting that every opinion uttered be original or value-adding. Ideas will sort themselves out. If everybody insists on being original before speaking out, it will be a very quiet meeting.
- What is wrong with disagreement? Wouldn't that lead to more robust exchanges?

CHAPTER 12

Part Four

Takada san emerged from his reflection and soul-searching with a clearer view of his responsibilities as a senior leader. While he still held on to his values as a Japanese, he was able to contribute more openly and assertively at global meetings. He did not stop there. He went on to share his experience with his Japanese colleagues. These days, his Japanese colleagues are much more willing to speak up and defend their ideas.

How Wise Leaders Encourage Group Reflection

In Chapter 5, we discussed how leaders can engage their people to create shared meaning and purpose. It is also possible during such sessions to encourage group reflection. Ikujiro Nonaka[7] and Hirotaka Takeuchi, two Japanese professors, have taught and lectured extensively about how leaders can foster practical wisdom in others. It is only through sharing life experiences and defining moments that will lead to distributed leadership. This is one of the biggest responsibilities of wise leaders.

In the US Army, there is a simple and yet practical way of conducting group reflection to extract lessons learnt after every operation. It is called the AAR (After Action Reviews).[8] In its simplest form, an AAR consists of three questions:

1. What happened?

2. What did we expect?

3. What can we learn from the gap?

Many large companies around the world have adopted the ARR as a process to identify best practices which they want to spread, and mistakes that they don't want to repeat. A cautionary note is in order. Conducting the AAR is only the first part. After discovering what the lessons are, the most important step is to apply the lessons learnt on current and future projects. Otherwise, the same mistakes will be discovered again and again.

How to Reflect

Reflection does not have to be done in any particular way. The only requisite is that there be a space of quiet in the midst of our busy existence. How we do it must fit in with our life and personality.

Some do it at the start of the day. Some prefer the solitude of a late night. Writing down one's thoughts in a journal is a common approach. Journaling has its uses and advantages. But it is not for everyone. Others may prefer to just do nothing in particular and let their thoughts home in what comes naturally. Then there are others who prefer to just work out at the gym, or partake in any other activities that give the brain a break, so to speak.

Some questions that can aid our reflection are as follows, and the reader can add to the list as they become more proficient in the art of reflection:

1. What can I learn from this incident?

2. What other perspectives are there?

3. Why did I react in this manner?

4. What are others saying that I am not picking up?

5. What is my intuition telling me?

6. How should I proceed now?

7. How consistent are my words and actions with my values and principles?

CHAPTER 12

Part Four

8. What if I am wrong?

9. What needs to be said that I am afraid of saying?

In Chapter 13, we move on to a topic of singular importance: self-renewal. Let's discover whether the mind can improve the body and vice-versa.

PRACTICES

Q1: In the story *The Rolling Stone*, Maugham said of his subject:

> *The insignificance of his mien was a true index to the insignificance of his soul. Behind the blank wall was blankness.*

Do you agree that a person's demeanour reveals much about who he is?

Q2: How can you apply the lessons of extraordinary people as synthesized by Gardner to your own life?

Chapter 13

SELF-RENEWAL

In order for man to succeed in life, God provided him with two means: education and physical activity. Not separately, one for the soul and the other for the body, but for the two together. With these two means, man can attain perfection.

Plato (427–347 BC)
Greek philosopher

The pace of work is unlikely to let up any time soon. Going by war stories that are circulating, a common pattern has emerged: an endless series of 12- to 14-hour workdays, mounting workload and stress, constant travelling, exhaustion, little family time, unhealthy meals, insufficient sleep, no time for exercise and weight gain. And consequently, health problems such as the following arise: hypertension, diabetes, chronic back pain, migraine, etc. Not only is there a physical toll, mentally, emotionally and spiritually, people are feeling depleted. And this has a deleterious impact, not only personally, but also on families and organizations. If leaders are in a bad state, how can they lead effectively?

Mind–Body Connection

Western medicine has long been dominated by the erroneous assumption[1] — attributed to famous 17th-century French philosopher and mathematician Rene Descartes — that the mind and body are two separate entities. This mechanistic view is known as Cartesian dualism or the Cartesian split. The conventional belief has been that the mind cannot directly improve bodily health. Western-trained medical practitioners have traditionally relied on either drugs or surgery, or both, to treat and prevent diseases. And this approach has been phenomenally successful, wiping out dreaded medical scourges and plagues. Human beings are able to live longer and in a more meaningful way.

Until a few decades ago, researchers, medical journals and practising physicians continued to ignore or discount the notion that the mind is also an essential component in healing of the body. In the 1970s, Dr Herbert Benson of Harvard Medical School conducted research that shows conclusively that the mind can indeed influence the body. Dr Benson reports:

> Your mind can actually change the way your body functions, for good or ill. This finding effectively does away with Descartes's mind–body separation.

In simple terms, there is now scientific proof that the mind can heal the body.

In contrast to the mechanistic Western view, the Eastern view of the world is organic. By Eastern, we are referring to the mythical philosophies of Hinduism, Buddhism and Daoism.

The ancient Chinese believed that their existence was closely tied to the universe. Traditional Chinese medicine (TCM) draws its inspiration from Daoism which views man as a holistic entity, i.e. it recognizes the mind–body connection. For instance, psychological factors known as the seven emotions — joy, anger, sadness, anxiety, pensiveness, fear and fright will interact with internal organs leading to disharmony patterns. TCM doctors will consider the whole person in their treatment of patients taking into account a variety of factors such as physical condition, age, lifestyle, medical history, career and mental state.

With the pioneering work done by Dr Benson and his colleagues in the last 40 years, we are thus seeing an increasing convergence of thoughts between Eastern and Western traditions and philosophies about human wellness. When these two great schools of learning and knowing intersect, there is much benefit that will be conferred on the world. In the words of Werner Heisenberg,[2] winner of the Nobel Prize in physics in 1932 and one of the founders of quantum mechanics,

> *It is probably true quite generally that in the history of human thinking the most fruitful developments frequently take place at those points where two different lines of thought meet.*

He explained further that such thoughts may emanate from different aspects of human experience, different eras, cultural environments or religious traditions. When convergence does take place, he felt that a breakthrough or a paradigm shift would occur.

We will now discuss how we may leverage the mind–body connection to maximize our well-being and elevate our performance in work and life.

CHAPTER 13

Part Four

How Stress Affects Us

In our daily lives, stress is a constant companion that refuses to go away. None of us can escape it. When we are under a lot of stress, we tense up, our judgement becomes erratic and we are short-fused. But while excessive stress can be destructive, there are positive aspects to it as well.

Stress comes about when two events interact simultaneously: an external stimulus called a stressor and the resulting emotional and physical responses. Usually when referring to stress, we mean the negative kind. Such kind of stress comes about when we are caught in rush-hour traffic, locked in a conflict with someone, facing intense pressure to raise prices in a competitive market, racing to meet a deadline that is rapidly approaching, and so on. In such a state of arousal, the primitive regions of our brain, the same areas that control eating, aggression and fear, get activated. Suddenly the nerve circuits ignite the body's fight-or-flight response as if we were facing a life-threatening event. Within ten milliseconds of sounding the alarm, an excess production of stress-hormone secretions such as adrenaline, norepinephrine and cortisol floods our body and brain.

The fight-or-flight response is the same ancient alarm that jump-started hunter–gatherers into evasive actions from a charging sabre-toothed tiger. This is a built-in gift of evolution without which we humans won't be here today. But there is a downside to this. This stress response is ill-suited for our modern life when the only threats are everyday events such as blowing a sales call or preparing for a major presentation. Yet, our mind is so powerful that we can set off the alarm just by thinking ourselves into a frenzy. And many of us are chronically under stress because we have become addicted to it and don't know how to manage it. When the stress pattern becomes routine, the constant biochemical pounding takes its toll and our mind–body system starts to wear out at an accelerated rate. This will result in high-blood pressure, heart attacks, strokes and diabetes.

Yerkes–Dodson Law

Stress, as we have alluded to earlier, is not all bad. The beneficial and harmful effects of stress on performance and efficiency were first described in 1908 by Robert M. Yerkes and John D. Dodson of Harvard Physiologic Laboratory. The Yerkes–Dodson Curve is shown below.

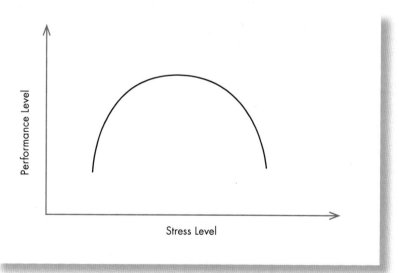

Both investigators demonstrated that as stress increases, so do efficiency and performance until it reaches a certain level. From that point onwards, when stress continues to build up, performance and efficiency decline dramatically. This is where the symptoms of excessive stress kick in. Not only is the mind–body system being attacked quietly and insidiously, such stress-related disorders surface: people can't think clearly, mistakes pile up, serious errors of judgement occur and people become hostile. In severe cases, panic sets in, depression and insomnia follow, causing emotional collapse.

As far back as 1983, *Time* magazine declared stress as an epidemic. Healthcare cost is rising and companies' bottom line is hurt as productivity drops. Just as importantly, the quality of life for workers and their families is adversely affected by illnesses and sudden disruption of their careers. However, as business executives and top-flight athletes have found out, stress can also be a stimulus for outstanding performance. Good stress, also called eustress, energizes and spurs us to outperform.

In an easygoing environment without pressure, well-defined objectives with deadlines and clear accountability, people get demotivated and even slack off. We all have met people who do their best work when the deadline is looming. When it is a do-or-die situation, team members put aside their differences and start to focus all their effort on attaining common goals. They may also think more clearly, become more decisive and innovative.

Being able to perform under pressure is a prized quality. But some managers have a misguided notion that if they pile on the pressure, their people will pull out all stops and deliver the best ideas, again and again. This is true to a certain point as Yerkes and Dodson discovered. Beyond that point, creativity becomes a casualty.

Creativity Under the Gun

Theresa Amabile[3] of Harvard Business School has spent nearly 40 years researching creativity. In the early 2000s, she did an extensive

CHAPTER 13

Part Four

study on knowledge workers in a number of companies working under extreme time pressure on projects that required high level of inventiveness. They involved companies in the consumer products, high-tech and chemical industries. Her research shows that under extreme stress, creativity ends up getting killed! She has reported that although time pressure may drive people to work more and get more done, and may even make them feel more creative, it actually is no more than an illusion.

She has also found no evidence to bolster the widespread belief that fear and sadness may stimulate creativity. On the contrary, people who are excited about their work and happy are more likely to be more creative. The literature on positive psychology makes a compelling case for helping people grow and remain energized at work. It can boost performance in a sustainable way.

In our contemporary workplace, however, pressure and unhappiness will be unavoidable. True, there is now greater awareness that companies need to avoid the negative impact of accumulated stress on their employees. But organizations, both profit and not-for-profit, will continue to be results oriented and drive their people to perform relentlessly. So, let's not hold our breath that work pace will slow down much. This will not happen in the West, much less the East. People will be expected to be creative and deliver while time-starved and under stress.

Learning How to Relax

When we feel stress is building up, what do we usually do? The sensible and more self-aware among us know that continuing to plug away is not going to do much good. We will soon run smack against the law of diminishing returns aka the Yerkes–Dodson law. Dr Benson has introduced nearly 40 years ago a simple, effective and scientifically proven way for us to combat stress, and not be a slave to the fight-or-flight response. This is called the *relaxation response* (RR).

As he points out, the basic elements in this technique have been known and used for millennia in many cultures, religions and ways of life throughout the world such as Christianity, Judaism, Islamic mysticism or Sufism, Hinduism, Daoism, Buddhism, Zen, Yoga and Shintoism. The relaxation response is now known as the Benson–Henry Protocol. These are the steps involved:

1. Pick a focus word, phrase, image or short prayer. Or focus only on your breathing during the exercise.

2. Find a quiet place and sit calmly in a comfortable position.

3. Close your eyes.

4. Progressively relax all your muscles.

5. Breathe slowly and naturally. As you exhale, repeat or picture silently your focus word or phrase, or simply focus on your breathing rhythm.

6. Assume a passive attitude. When other thoughts intrude, simply think, "Oh well" and return to your focus.

7. Continue with this exercise for an average of 15 to 20 minutes.

8. Practise this technique at least once daily.

The clinical work by Benson and other doctors and researchers has shown that the relaxation response is an effective therapy for anxiety, mild and moderate depression, undue anger and hostility, insomnia, hypertension and a whole host of other stress-related disorders. Specifically, these are the benefits:

CHAPTER 13

Part Four

- Decreased metabolism, heart rate, blood pressure and rate of breathing.
- Calming in brain activity.
- Increase in attention and decision-making functions of the brain.
- Changes in gene activity that are the opposite of those associated with stress.

In short, RR is a practice that we should learn and apply in our daily work and life. It is our natural defence against the pernicious effect of stress that literally tears us apart mentally, physically and emotionally. It is also a technique that prevents us from being overwhelmed and swamped by countless stimuli coming at us simultaneously. By habitually breaking away for a few precious minutes, RR allows us to take a breather and regain our perspective. We gain resilience because we remain clear-eyed and clear-minded in the midst of confusion.

What Can Organizations Do?

Senior executives in organizations can start by understanding the ideas described in this chapter:

- The fight-or-flight response
- The Yerkes–Dodson law
- Theresa Amabile's findings that creativity dies under pressure
- The relaxation response

Piling on pressure unnecessarily is a habit that bosses need to mindfully rein in. I have known bosses who take perverse pride in working 14-hour days, and expect their people to do likewise. Some will send emails in the middle of the night, while declaring in a half-mocking way that they do not expect underlings to work like

CHAPTER 13

Part Four

they do. In some companies, especially in Asia, nobody leaves the office unless the boss has gone home. Dilbert has some interesting things to say about such managers in the following cartoon.[4]

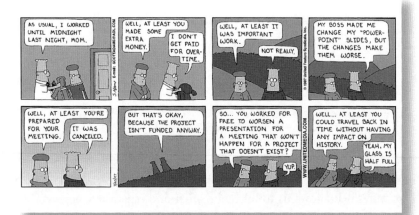

Exercise Can Supercharge the Brain

Dr Benson's work has conclusively shown that the mind can heal the body. Can the body in turn heal the mind? The answer is a resounding yes. This is the mind–body connection in full cycle. John R. Ratey[5] is a professor of psychiatry at Harvard Medical School. In 2008, his book *Spark: The Revolutionary New Science of Exercise and the Brain* was published. In it, he shared the latest research that for our brain to function at its peak, we need to engage in aerobic exercises. He explained how physical exercise improves mood and attention, lowers stress and anxiety, helps stave off addiction, controls the sometimes tumultuous effects of hormonal changes and guards against and even reverses some of the effects of aging on the brain.

Generally, all of us who exercise regularly feel much better afterwards, but we may not know what makes it so. Perhaps it is because we are burning off fat or stress or reducing our muscle tensions. Or boosting endorphins. Dr Ratey explains that the real reason we feel great when we get our blood pumping is that it makes our brain functions at its best. In his view, the benefit of physical activity to the brain is far more important than what it does for the body. He continues:

> Building muscle and conditioning the heart and lungs are essentially side effects. I often tell my patients that the point of exercise is to build and condition the brain.

Neuroscientists now have evidence to show that our brain works just as muscles do. It grows with use, and withers with inactivity. This revolutionary idea is called neuroplasticity. In other words, the maxim "Use it or lose it" applies equally to our brains and muscles.

Psychiatrist and psychoanalyst Norman Doidge[6] has written an inspiring book about the endless adaptability of the human brain. In it, he shares incredible case histories of a 90-year-old doctor who is still practising medicine, the stroke victim who learned to move and talk again and blind people helped to see, intelligence quotients raised and memories sharpened, etc. Doidge says:

> Nothing speeds brain atrophy more than being immobilized in the same environment; the monotony undermines our dopamine and attentional systems crucial to maintaining brain plasticity.

He recommends that to preserve brain health, we should immerse ourselves in a cognitively rich physical environment in which new

CHAPTER 13

Part Four

motor skills such as dances and tai chi are acquired. People should continue learning new things such as a foreign language, play a musical instrument or even enrol in an academic programme.

Growing older is not an inevitable process of decline and decay, as many younger people think. Older people can develop new skills and are often wiser and more socially adept than they were as younger adults. Pablo Casals was one of the greatest cellists of all time. When he was 91 years old, he was approached by a student who asked, "Master, why do you continue to practise?" He replied, "Because I am making progress."

In the penultimate chapter of this book, we will meet Sir Arthur Conan Doyle, the creator of fictional detective Sherlock Holmes. He kicks off our discussion about the hidden gems in our brain attic. How do we extract them when we need them most, given that the gems are buried together with all the other clutter and trivia that we have amassed over the years?

PRACTICES

Q1: How can you counteract workplace stress so that you can stay healthy and calm?

Q2: We know that creativity dies under the gun. Yet, today's pressure-cooker work environment will not ameliorate. How, then, will you protect the creative side of your people?

GEMS
IN THE BRAIN ATTIC

*The unexpected has happened so continually in my life
that it has ceased to deserve the name.*

Sir Arthur Conan Doyle (1859–1930)
Scottish physician, writer and
creator of Sherlock Holmes

There is a story of Archimedes that most of us are familiar with. In 265 BC, King Hiero II of Syracuse commissioned a goldsmith to craft for him a golden crown as an offering to the gods. When the crown was delivered to him, he was delighted. However, he soon heard rumours that the crown might not be of pure gold. The goldsmith could have cheated him by using an alloy of gold and silver. Being a fair-minded person, he wanted to find out the truth before reacting. He then turned to his cousin Archimedes, who, at the tender age of 22, was already famous for his work in mathematics, mechanics and physics. Archimedes mulled long and hard over this problem. One afternoon, he went to the public bath as was the common practice in those days. While going through the ritual of cleansing and scrubbing himself, he stepped into a tub of water. As he observed the water overflowing upon his immersion into the tub, he had an epiphany. As gold is denser than silver, a given weight of pure gold will displace less water than an alloy. In his excitement, he sprang out and streaked naked through the streets of Syracuse yelling *Eureka!* which means *I have found it*. This was how he stumbled upon what is now known as the Archimedes's Principle. Soon he demonstrated to the king that he had indeed been duped as the crown displaced more water than an equal weight of gold.

There have been many *Eureka* moments in the annals of mankind. When they occur, they lead to monumental discoveries that change the course of history. Such instances are, however, few and far between. A humbler and more common variant is the countless unheralded instances of ordinary people who chance upon new ways of seeing things in the course of their daily lives. Such unexpected insights do help individuals, companies and society become more creative.

The Sherlock Holmes Method

The fictitious Sherlock Holmes[1] is probably the world's most famous detective. Although it has been more than 100 years, Holmes continues to delight readers around the world with his extraordinary powers of thoughts and observation. When he first met Dr Watson, the man who would become his faithful sidekick and biographer, he said that he considered a person's brain to be like an attic. Hence, one had to stock it with such furniture as would be useful. If one were foolish enough to take in all kinds of useless information, what might be useful might be jumbled up with the rest of the junk. And rather pompously he would intone,

> *... the skilful workman is very careful indeed as to what he takes into his brain attic.*

Paradoxically, however, Holmes always proudly proclaimed,

> *You know my method. It is founded upon the observation of trifles.*

Yet, Holmes has never failed to pierce through the fog, and unravel countless cases and mysteries that left others completely befuddled. But even for the great detective nothing is always smooth sailing. There are numerous cases when he draws a blank. That is when he plays the violin and smokes his pipe as an escape from his highly advanced cognitive processes. Then suddenly, he has got it and is up and running with Watson in tow.

A Sudden Flash of Insight

Here are some examples of how a flash of insight or the *Aha* moments may strike at the most unexpected times:

- A senior government leader Maggie was feeling anxious about a meeting that would take place in a few days' time with the country's top political leaders to review a rather controversial policy paper that she and her team had prepared. A lot was riding on getting a resounding endorsement. They had worked on it long and hard.

CHAPTER 14

Part Four

Now the day was fast approaching. She suddenly felt a knot in her stomach. Something didn't feel right. Could the pitch be made more compelling? She tried brainstorming with her people but that didn't get them far. Not wanting to alarm them, she decided to stay calm and disengaged from further discussions. On the night before the meeting she continued to be antsy. It was too late to make any changes now. Close to physical and mental exhaustion, she knew that she had to unwind. She reached for her hi-fi system and played her favourite classical piece. Lost in the music, she felt herself relaxing for the first time in two weeks. All of a sudden, all the key pieces of the presentation started to fit together like a jigsaw.

- At the end of a gruelling day of discussions, Jong was glad to be back home. Before dinner, he laced up his running shoes and went for a jog. When he neared the end of the long and winding trail, he could feel the tenseness in his body melting away. Heading back home, he suddenly felt uneasy. What was it? Luckily he had his mobile phone with him. A quick check confirmed that he had a telecall in 30 minutes' time. In the flurry of the day's activities, he had clean forgotten this appointment.

- Another commonly encountered situation is one that many of us will identify with. We run into an old friend whom we have not met for many years. As we talk, we are trying desperately to recall her name. No, it just doesn't come to our mind. Later that evening, her name suddenly barges into our consciousness when we are watching television. The same frustrating event plays out in other variations such as recalling the title of a movie, tune, book, etc.

Eliciting the *Eureka* Moments

All of us work hard at our job. Yet, we lament that we aren't reaping the returns that we desire in terms of fresh ideas, let alone *Eureka* or *Aha* moments. What if there is a simple and scientifically proven technique that we can tap into at will to evoke new insights, to see fresh perspectives that have eluded us and others?

In researching this book, I have found that through the ages, thinkers, scientists, philosophers and poets have always been fascinated by the mystical and magical facility *to peer up into the night sky and see a faint star twinkling while equally intelligent colleagues see only darkness.*[2] And in the last few decades, academics in fields ranging from anthropology to neuroscience have been similarly intrigued and engaged.

In describing what leads to sudden flashes of illumination, most are quick to admit that breakthroughs do not seem to evolve linearly from analysis. For instance, Dr Edgar Mitchell, American astronaut and the sixth man on the moon, speaks reverently of the mysterious process that lies outside our consciousness. When the conditions are right, they spring forth from hunches buried deep in the recesses of our mind.

Dr Herbert Benson — he has taught us much about safeguarding our mental, emotional and physical health through the relaxation response in Chapter 13 — has gone on to research how we may evoke the *Eureka* moments. This has led to what he calls the *Breakout Principle*, a simple and scientifically proven technique that we can all use with great benefits to ourselves and our organizations.

The Breakout Principle[3]

Dr Benson's Breakout Principle is the culmination of four decades of original scientific work at Harvard Medical School. There is a distinct four-stage process:

1. Struggle

2. Release

3. Breakout/peak experience

4. New normal state

The four-stage process is shown in diagrammatic form below.

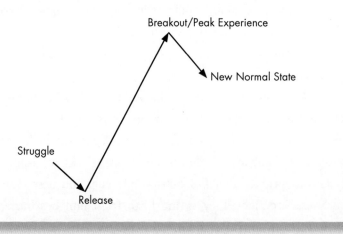

Stage 1: The struggle

First and foremost, no breakout is possible without a struggle. Imagine ourselves grappling with a particularly intractable problem — a new product launch to significantly gain on the competition, a new approach to tackle severe traffic congestion in the metropolis, writing the score for a musical, choosing whom to hire between two outstanding job candidates, etc. These had transpired: collection of tonnes of data, analysis *ad nauseam*, never-ending discussions and changes. And we become anxious, pressurized and ill-humoured. Our blood pressure goes up, our heart races and we are gripped by the fight-or-flight response. The stress creeps up quickly along the Yerkes–Dodson curve.

Stage 2: The release

As we press on, there reaches a point when we are hitting the wall. I know that I am at this stage when I sense that m*y brain is getting fried!* Others feel their shoulders are starting to ache and they just can't sit still any more. That is when we are near the top of the Yerkes–Dodson curve. Continuing to sweat away will be counterproductive. We must now, even if involuntarily, make our escape by walking away, letting go or just abandoning the struggle. In the examples cited earlier, the escape takes various forms such as

1. Archimedes going to the bathing house,

2. Sherlock Homes smoking his pipe and drawing on his violin,

3. Maggie abandoning all cares and immersing in the lyrical strains of her favourite violin concerto and

4. Jong going for his jog through the woods.

In all these instances, the mode of escape disrupted the thought patterns that had those involved spinning around in circles. Stage 2 is no more than applying the relaxation response discussed in Chapter 13. Benson reminds us that it will take about

CHAPTER 14

Part Four

an average of 15 to 20 minutes. When we abandon the struggle, our neurons start to fire in different patterns and this becomes the foundation for new insights. As our brain quietens down, a series of biochemical *explosions* will begin to bubble up inside our body and brain. Benson attributes this to the release of increasing amounts of nitric oxide throughout the body. There is also a remarkable calming of body and mind as shown by fMRI (functional magnetic resonance imaging) graphs.

Stage 3: Breakout/Peak experience

This is when the breakout occurs — the *Eureka* moment at the end of a gruelling intellectual journey. Elite athletes, artists and dancers reach this stage when they train hard and then let go and allow the spirit of the moment to take charge. Psychologist Mihaly Csikszentmihalyi calls this moment the *flow*. The Dao again:

> In the eye of the storm,
> Can you stay centred and calm?
> Having done all that is possible,
> Can you sit and let go?

When flow occurs, the right stroke or movement happens by itself, effortlessly, and without conscious thought. The golfer and the swing become one. We can't tell the dancer from the dance, the words appear spontaneously on the writer's computer screen.

Stage 4: Returning to a new normal state

The breakout cycle ends by creating a new baseline for performance. This means that the struggle is remembered and leaves the person in a stronger position to elicit breakouts in future. The more the habit of eliciting breakout is practised, the more natural it will become.

Adopting a Creative Ritual

Friends who read the early draft of this book have posed an interesting question. They observed that some people seem to be more creative than the rest of us despite being constantly busy and on the go. Is there some discipline or process that they might have adopted? Thomas Edison was most prescient when he said,

> *Genius is one percent inspiration, ninety-nine percent perspiration.*

Howard Gardner studied the lives of extraordinary people and has concluded that talent by itself is not enough. Being outstanding will require *years and years of sustained effort*, and being deeply passionate and curious and always aiming a bit higher every day. This deliberate practice isn't the kind of hard work that parents tell their kids about. It takes decades. It is difficult. It hurts. More than talent, it is the true path of great performance.[4]

Twyla Tharp,[5] one of America's greatest choreographers, has this advice for us all:

> *Creativity is not a gift from the gods bestowed by some divine and mystical spark. It is the production of preparation and effort and it's within reach of all of us. All it takes is the willingness to make creativity a habit, an integral part of your life.*

To her, sustained creativity begins with rituals, self-knowledge, harnessing one's memories and relying on a series of immensely

CHAPTER 14

Part Four

practical exercises that she has developed over a lifetime to help her get out of a rut. Here are some examples of creative rituals:

- Twyla Tharp says that she knows her day will be a productive one by waking up at 5:30am, putting on her workout clothes and hailing a cab to the gym. Once she does that, all will be well.

- A journalist wills himself to write when he sits before his notebook. He will not wait for inspiration. He does not get up and wander around until the words have started flowing. He rejects the notion of the writer's block.

- A senior business leader who needs to speak frequently to various audiences, both inside and outside his company, will prepare his script carefully. Then he will internalize the key themes and rehearse his talk a few times. When he stands before his audience, he will throw away his script and speak off the cuff. This has worked very well for him. Though he sometimes forgets some key points, he is unfazed. He has over the years developed a flair for improvisation. Very importantly, his audience feels that he is connecting with them authentically. And he is able to get his key points across impactfully.

Here is my favourite example. It is about the Everyman or Everywoman. We see this person in all walks of life. One such person whom I know very well describes his creative ritual as follows:

Life is full of ups and downs. Sometimes if I am lucky, there are more ups than downs. Other times, I have more downs than ups.

I am used to it. It has never been a breeze for me. Not in my childhood, in school, in college and not at work.

I do my very best and never give up. I know collaboration and diversity are critical to success. I also know as a leader, I have to take risks. Otherwise, why am I given this responsibility?

In my company, we focus on making things happen so that everybody benefits. We don't ever rest on our laurels. If we succeed today, we congratulate ourselves for a while, have a drink and laugh a little. Then tomorrow the teams get together to do things even better.

It is a culture of trying new ideas and constant experimentation. Failure is a constant companion. But we always learn from it and recover.

And now the journey is ending. One more chapter and we are there. Let's explore how we are able to listen to our inner voice and stay mindful throughout our lives.

PRACTICES

Q1: Are there gems in your brain attic? What treasures have you excavated of late? How has it happened?

Q2: What is your creative ritual?

Q3: How will you help your people become more creative?

Part Four   CHAPTER 14

MINDFULNESS

---

*Choice of attention — to pay attention to this
and ignore that — is to the inner life what choice
of action is to the outer. In both cases man is
responsible for his choice and must accept
the consequences. As Ortega y Gasset said:
"Tell me what you pay attention to, and
I will tell you who you are."*

W.H. Auden (1907–1973)
Anglo-American poet

In Chapter 4, we learnt from Viktor Frankl an immensely
important principle for living meaningfully. It is the concept
of choice of response to whatever we encounter in our lives.
To recap, this is what Frankl taught:

*Between stimulus and response, there is a space. In
that space lies our freedom and our power to choose our
response. In our response lies our growth and happiness.*

As the poet Auden points out, this is but for the outer realm of our existence. Then there is the inner life. How do we live our inner life, i.e. what do we choose to focus on day in and day out? If choice of response and action defines our destiny, then choice of attention defines who we are.

What Is Mindfulness?

Being conscious of how we choose to pay attention is the practice of mindfulness. Although mindfulness originates from Buddhism, it has profound relevance for our present-day lives regardless of our culture, creed and persuasion. Mindfulness is a state of being fully present, aware of ourselves and others, and sensitive to how we are reacting to our environment. Leaders who are mindful will be more effective in understanding and relating to others, as well as motivating them towards a shared purpose. This is closely related to EQ or emotional intelligence.

In their book *Resonant Leadership*, Richard Boyatzis[1] and Annie McKee explain that to live mindfully means that we are constantly and consciously in tune with ourselves — listening carefully to our bodies, minds, hearts and spirits. When we attend to ourselves in such a manner, we become aware about what matters most to us. It allows us to engage our passion and stay positive emotionally. More importantly, we are in touch with our inner sentinel. We quickly sense it when we are about to veer down the wrong path such as compromising our values, making a bad judgement call or ignoring our health. Mindful living means we are guided by our inner voice — a voice that draws upon intuition, wisdom and a subtle yet sophisticated assessment of what goes on around us.

Another important aspect of mindfulness is having compassion for oneself, without which it is very difficult to feel genuine

CHAPTER 15

Part Four

compassion for others. An example of a leader who lived mindfully was Yang whom we met in Chapter 2. If you recall, his company — like many others — was reeling from the Lehman Brothers financial debacle. The Executive Committee at New Jersey went into a panic mode. The order was to let people go across the global operations in order to cut cost. Yang was head of the Southeast Asian business which was doing well. Yet, his boss Don callously instructed that business performance was not to be considered. It was just cut and slash. To make matters worse, the boss also made it clear that in order to safeguard intellectual property, none of the employees affected were to be told in advance. Just round them up, ask them to hand over their employee badges and have Security escort them out of the company's premises.

Yang was caught between a rock and a hard place. While he knew that protecting intellectual property was important, he felt that treating his staff with respect and compassion was just as essential. And despite the tremendous pressure he was under, Yang kept his cool. It was his defining moment. He reflected deeply, and sought the counsel of close friends and family members. Then he decided to lead with his head, heart and guts. The rest he left to providence. Making his choices mindfully, he attended to the emotional needs of the people whom he had to lay off. Although that put him on collision course with his boss, he was unfazed. Today, the hurt and distress of the sudden layoff is in the distant past. But how Yang stood up for the people and led with authenticity is a source of inspiration for his colleagues.

Going Through Life on Autopilot

Jon Kabat-Zinn[2] is Professor of Medicine Emeritus and founding director of the Stress Reduction Clinic and the Center for

Mindfulness in Medicine, Health Care, and Society at the University of Massachusetts Medical School. He explains that in the course of our day, it is common for us to momentarily lose touch with ourselves and with the full extent of our possibilities.

This is the opposite of mindfulness. It turns into mindlessness. When this happens, we start to see, think and act in a robot-like fashion. By failing to be in touch with what is deepest in ourselves, we forego our greatest opportunities for learning and growing. If we do not awaken to our senses, we will lead the life of a zombie on earth. Here are some examples of going through life on autopilot that may sound familiar.

Case 1

MULTITASKING   Countless people at work do this because they believe that it will help them get many things done simultaneously. Isn't it an inescapable aspect of modern-day work that things all happen so quickly that multitasking is a survival skill? This is an example of the herd instinct. Everybody seems to be doing it so we should do it as well. And it can't be that wrong, can it?

The first thing wrong about multitasking is the assumption that our attention is infinite. It isn't. We don't really multitask. What we really do is to rapidly shift our attention from task to task. There are two counterproductive effects. First, the quality of our work suffers and we are actually less productive. Second, we start to develop inner frenzy and have difficulties staying organized, setting priorities and managing our

CHAPTER 15

Part Four

attention. Indeed, we start to behave in a robot-like manner not only in our work but also in our relationships. Even smart people[3] who overload their mental circuits will underperform!

A study[4] conducted in 2001 by Joshua Rubinstein, Jeffrey Evans and David Meyer found that participants lost significant amounts of time as they switched between multiple tasks and lost even more time as the tasks became increasingly complex. The March 2013 edition of *Harvard Business Review*[5] has a report called "The Multitasking Paradox". Its advice for mindless multitaskers: stick to one thing at a time; you will get more done.

Case 2

LOSING TOUCH WITH WHO WE ARE   We first met Ronnie in Chapter 3. He was the person who finally landed the coveted post of President Asia-Pacific at KDC, a European multinational, after 15 years of hard work. Here was an extremely capable and dedicated executive who reached the pinnacle of his career and then proceeded to unravel. His rise and fall wasn't all that surprising.

Like so many highly-driven people, he was single-minded in pursuit of his ambition. Excelling and moving up was the be-all and end-all. Everything else was irrelevant. There wasn't a larger purpose apart from this. Losing touch with his real self right at the start, he became an automaton. Ironically, when he finally attained his dream job, his derailment process started on cue, as though it had been programmed into his life script.

The Practice of Meditation

How does one live mindfully? It starts with us finding a space of inner quiet regularly in our day. Kabat-Zinn[6] explains that in the course of our day, ordinary thoughts and impulses run through our mind like a coursing river. Having a space of inner quiet will enable us to learn how to get out of this river temporarily, sit on its bank and listen to it, learn from it and then use its energies to guide us rather than tyrannize us. This process doesn't magically happen by itself. It takes commitment and dedication. The way to cultivate our ability to be in the present moment is through meditation.

Meditation is tremendously difficult and takes a lifetime of practice. For a start, try the following exercise that Kabat-Zinn recommends:

- Once in a while throughout the day, try pausing and sitting down.
- Be aware of your breathing for as short as five minutes or even five seconds.
- How does the present moment feel? What seems to be happening around you?
- Whatever it is, just accept the present moment. Don't try to change anything.
- Stay calm. Continue to breathe and let go. Breathe and let go …
- Give yourself permission to be in touch with what is *now*. There is nothing to change.

Kabat-Zinn says the moment will come when you know you are ready. That's when you should move in the direction your heart tells you, mindfully and with resolution.

CHAPTER 15

Part Four

Riding the Ox Home

In Zen Buddhism,[7] there is a parable about seeking enlightenment. It is depicted by a series of ten pictures in which a young ox-herder struggles through various stages in coming to terms with an ox. This is a metaphor of a leader seeking to understand his true self. In the final picture, the ox-herder sits astride the ox's back, blissfully playing a child's tune on a bamboo flute. He is entering the marketplace, at peace with himself.

As a conclusion to this book, I would like to leave you with an image of the ox-herder. This was photographed at the site of Borobudur, the 9th century Buddhist temple in Magelang, Central Java in Indonesia. I thank you for the privilege of accompanying you on your leadership journey. Hopefully you will agree that the shortest trip home is a circuitous route.

PRACTICES

Q1: If you have not done so yet, do check out the custodian–explorer continuum diagnostic in Appendix 1. What will you do to enhance your ability to lead like an explorer?

Q2: How mindful are you as a leader? What are some personal examples of mindfulness or mindlessness?

Q3: Ronnie is an archetype of a talented person consumed by his burning ambition. There are countless such people around us. Perhaps he reminds us of someone we know? What could have saved Ronnie from himself?

Q4: In Appendix 2 we discuss healthcare services, which are heading towards crisis proportions globally. I feature two healthcare practitioners who have decided to make a difference by turning conventional medical practices on its head. Can you do the same within your own field?

Q5: In Appendix 3, I have collated all the questions at the end of each chapter into one document. This serves as a refresher of topics discussed in the book. How many of these questions are pertinent to you?

DISCOVER THE HIDDEN EXPLORER IN YOU

This diagnostic is a quick way to assess where you are in the custodian–explorer continuum. Score yourself according to the way you behave between each pair of statements in the assessment. If you score in the lower half of the range in any given pair, that may be a good place to focus on. Raising awareness of how we lead and behave currently is the first step in engendering a more creative climate. With practice, the explorer's DNA can be cultivated.

The Custodian	1	2	3	4	5	6	7	The Explorer
1. Seek to establish order and clarity	1	2	③	4	5	6	7	**1.** Encourage experimentation and improvisation
2. Practical and results-oriented	1	2	③	4	5	6	7	**2.** Imaginative and counterintuitive
3. Value logical and practical people	1	2	3	4	5	⑥	7	**3.** Value people who see opportunities in uncertainties and ambiguities
4. Rely on data and analytics to make decisions	1	2	3	4	5	6	⑦	**4.** Will decide despite incomplete and unreliable information
5. Always focused and action-oriented	1	②	3	4	5	6	7	**5.** Always listening to divergent perspectives from many sources
6. Respected for consistently delivering results	1	2	③	4	5	6	7	**6.** Possess credibility to win support for unconventional ideas
7. Network within the same business space	1	2	3	4	5	6	⑦	**7.** Network across business boundaries and sectors
8. Stay ahead of the competition by adapting, and driving changes	①	2	3	4	5	6	7	**8.** Leapfrog the competition through disruption
9. Ask: What? How? How much? When?	1	2	3	4	5	6	⑦	**9.** Ask: Why? Why Not? What if? Who?
10. When uncertain, unwilling to say, "I don't know."	1	2	3	4	⑤	6	7	**10.** When uncertain, comfortable saying, "I don't know."
11. Slow to confront reality when things don't pan out	1	2	3	4	5	6	⑦	**11.** Quick to confront reality when things don't pan out
12. Always looking outwards to spot trends	1	2	3	4	⑤	6	7	**12.** Intuitively know what lies on the horizon

LEADING CREATIVELY IN HEALTHCARE SERVICES

In the world's richest countries, healthcare spending represents one of the biggest areas of expenditure. And it is expected to rise rapidly in the years ahead due to aging populations, increasing chronic diseases and the development of newer and more costly treatments. According to the United Nations, population aging is unprecedented and without parallel in the history of humanity. A silver-haired tsunami is on its way.

In the United States, Europe and Japan, 13, 17 and 23 per cent of people are aged over 65, respectively. And in Singapore and Hong Kong, the percentages are 9 and 13, respectively. Fast forward to 2030. More than 55 countries are expected to have their 65 and older populations at 20 per cent of their total. Singapore and Hong Kong will join Japan with more than a quarter of their people above 65!

The Looming Global Healthcare Crisis

The national healthcare systems around the world are under tremendous strain. Many countries, such as those in Western Europe, have a policy of universal coverage which means that all citizens enjoy full and comprehensive healthcare coverage with minimal out-of-pocket expenditure. Such universal coverage is

mostly achieved by state-mandated social insurance schemes or through taxes.

With healthcare costs now spiralling out of control, the notion of universal coverage is increasingly being questioned around the world. Although undoubtedly humane, they are an enormous drain on national resources and are unsustainable in the long term.[1] Nothing comes for free. Someone has to pay for it. For instance, Denmark has perhaps Europe's most generous welfare benefits.[2] The Danes get a cradle-to-grave safety net that includes free healthcare, a free university education and hefty handouts even to their richest citizens. Denmark has among the highest marginal income-tax rates in the world, with the top bracket of 57 per cent applied to incomes above US$80,000. Many Danes are convinced that they are heading down a slippery slope as the country's work ethic is already undermined. They are calling for an overhaul of its welfare system to wean people off government benefits.

Apart from aging populations, perverse incentives are also contributing factors. In describing the situation in the United States, Robert S. Kaplan and Michael E. Porter, both dons at Harvard Business School, said in a September 2011 *Harvard Business Review*[3] article:

> *The remedy to the cost crisis does not require medical science breakthroughs or new governmental regulations. It simply requires a new way to accurately measure costs and compare them with outcomes.*

Third-party payers (insurance companies and governments) reimburse for procedures performed rather than outcomes achieved, and patients bear little responsibility for the cost of healthcare services they demand. This leads to the so-called buffet syndrome.

Experts on healthcare systems recommend an integrated approach[4] as the future for healthcare. This means addressing the currently fragmented state of affairs. When different care providers are acting independently and in an uncoordinated manner, treatment becomes inefficient, frustrating and confusing for both patients and medical practitioners. There may be an over-reliance on costly specialist care and lengthy hospital stays. It can also sometimes lead to unnecessary and duplicative tests that put patients through emotional and financial strains, and delays in timely diagnosis and treatment.

The definition of integration varies among countries, but basically, the idea is to be able to offer coordinated care across the whole patient journey. Integration can be driven by payers such as insurers or governments. In many Western countries, there are already good examples of both insurer-led and government-led integration models.

A growing body of evidence suggests that the quality of healthcare is improved and costs reduced significantly if health-care provision is well integrated.[5] However, despite more success stories from countries embarking on reforms, most healthcare models around the world are still struggling with integration. In the following text, I feature two healthcare leaders who challenge conventional medical practices to reinvent the healthcare models in their respective countries: Singapore and India.

Reinventing the Singapore Model

Professor Philip Choo is CEO of Singapore's Tan Tock Seng Hospi-tal (TTSH). Meeting him recently at his office, Prof Choo explained to me he was greatly concerned about the state of healthcare in Singapore. Singapore's current hospital-centric healthcare system, as

with most countries, is just too costly. It is great at acute episodic care such as attending to someone who is a road accident victim, but lousy for those living with longstanding chronic diseases, like stroke and heart failure. He stressed:[6]

> I know I am on a failed model. Today, we wait for patients with problems to come to us. It is akin to operating a factory with an array of machines. We don't devote sufficient resources on preventive maintenance. When the equipment breaks down suddenly, we rush into action. This is a poor way of running a factory, much less a nation's healthcare system. The whole production system is disrupted when machines malfunction. Customer orders can't be filled. There is great stress on personnel. Emergency repairs are very costly. In healthcare, we need to be proactive. Break that cycle of emergency response and start to put in resources to maintain the health of the population. Otherwise, we will end up broke, just like where the rest of the world is today.

Currently, Singapore ranks sixth in the world in healthcare outcomes, yet spends proportionately less on healthcare than any other high-income country. As a percentage of gross domestic product, Singapore's healthcare expenditure is 4 per cent. This is less than one-fourth that in the United States and half that of Western European countries. It is also lower compared to that of Japan, South Korea, Taiwan and Hong Kong. In 2030, with one in four people reaching 65 years and above, what then? Will Singapore be able to afford the spike in healthcare spending as a nation?

Applying engineering principles to healthcare

Toyota has long been hailed as the world's best manufacturer of automobiles. In the last few decades, thousands of executives from various businesses around the world have toured Toyota's plants in Japan and in the United States to learn about the famed Toyota Production System (TPS). What is curious is that although Toyota has been extraordinarily open about its practices, few companies in fields as diverse as aerospace, consumer products, metal processing and industrial products have been able to replicate Toyota's success.

How can we decode the DNA of the TPS? Visitors usually walk away deeply impressed with the tools and practices on the assembly floors such as *kanban*, 5S, *jidoka*, etc. But this is only part of the story. There is an inherent paradox that most will miss. While the TPS epitomizes activities, connections and process flows that are rigidly scripted, at the same time, Toyota's operations are enormously flexible and adaptable. As alluded to in Chapter 8, it is contradictions that drive Toyota's success. Employees extract innovation through the creative tension between "thinking within the box" and a culture that encourages them to constantly challenge and improve existing systems. This creates a momentum that becomes self-generative.

In the early 2000s, Singapore healthcare administrators visited the Toyota Motomachi plant in Japan. After their study, they decided to adopt the TPS philosophy and framework to design *a hassle-free* experience for patients and visitors to their cluster of hospitals. They first started with Alexandra Hospital. Since then other public hospitals have also gone the Toyota way. In researching this case study, I was taken on a tour of Khoo Teck Puat Hospital (KTPH) by its CEO Chew Kwee Tiang. What I observed were not only the tools and processes of the TPS but also the focus on the cultural aspects: developing and empowering people, the foundation of a learning organization, collaboration and a collegial environment.

One of the most important pillars underpinning the TPS is *kaizen*. *Kaizen* is the Japanese concept of continuous improvement. The basis of *kaizen* is standardized work. You begin by creating a standard process using established best-known practices. Then you train others to apply this standardized process while continuously seeking ways to improve it further.

In the past four years, Prof Choo has been busy introducing standardization of healthcare procedures like assembly lines and categorization of patients like car models. Initially, there was a storm of protest from his colleagues. To them, it was sheer heresy. As he explains it,

> *Standardization in healthcare is unheard of and counterintuitive to healthcare workers. Weren't we all taught to treat all patients as individuals and offer them the individualized care that they deserve?*

But from another perspective, why shouldn't healthcare follow and benefit from proven business principles that reduce waste and raise efficiency? In the best-run service organizations around the world such as the Disney theme parks and hotels and airlines, staff have all been trained to deliver high-quality service in a personalized manner. He adds:

> *Standardization does not detract from caring for patients as individuals. You take what is best after research and experimentation and standardize it. It's the highest common denomination, not the lowest. So everybody benefits from the best practices. Can you imagine a pilot of an airline going through his pre-flight safety procedures with no standardization? Some days, he does this much and other days he does less. We'll be horrified!*

Using the data on 350,000 patients in his National Healthcare Group, Prof Choo categorizes them into five groups — *well, simple, complicated, serious* and *frail.* His aim is to maintain patients within each category as far as possible. The proportion of *well* can be increased through greater awareness and education about leading a healthy lifestyle. It is best to start young, and there is no better place than in the schools. Even those in the *simple* and *complicated* categories can avoid hospital admissions through consciously modifying their lifestyle habits such as giving up smoking, exercising regularly, eating wisely, not drinking and losing weight. In addition, healthcare providers can support patients through home visits or telephone follow-ups. Admissions for the *serious* group can be reduced by actively managing their medical condition. Intensive care can be provided to prevent worsening of the *frail.*

By adopting this targeted approach, the cost of healthcare will be reduced significantly while raising the outcome and improving the quality of life for the population. The cost of healthcare support for the five categories is shown in the following graph. Now more than a third of patients who used to be admitted for costly hospital treatment are diverted to other settings. Close to 70 per cent of all surgical procedures are now done as day surgery. Patients who used to stay up to three days in hospitals now stay only for a day, thereby freeing up beds for others. When their condition stabilizes, they are funnelled into community hospitals. This means more patients will receive rehabilitative support in primary care closer to their homes. As the capabilities at nursing homes are being enhanced through the presence of medical teams, patients can be treated there as well.

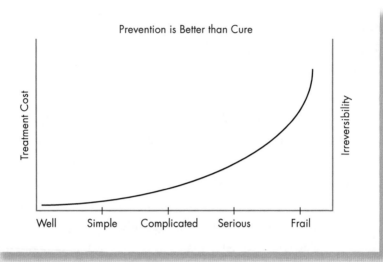

Prevention is Better than Cure

Treatment Cost

Irreversibility

Well   Simple   Complicated   Serious   Frail

Fix It When It Ain't Broke

In parallel with the effort to take an integrated healthcare delivery approach, the Singapore healthcare financing framework is also being reviewed. The framework treats the majority of healthcare consumers as co-paying partners together with the government, while making special provisions for the minority who cannot afford the co-payment. A co-payment philosophy encourages people to take accountability for leading a healthy lifestyle, and inculcates the ethos of self-reliance. In addition, it will not provide the rich with healthcare handouts that will be the case under a universal healthcare system.

With an aging population, there will need to be greater provision and flexibility to alleviate high out-of-pocket expenses that people will incur. Prof Choo mentions that the integrated healthcare system is still in its early days. The path to integration will be difficult given the existing divide between public and private sectors, general practitioners and specialists, and hospitals and community-based care.

He is convinced that the best time to act is before something is broken. It is his aim that within his lifetime, he is able to see the reformed model working, offering high quality, and financially sustainable, healthcare for all people in Singapore.

Performing Heart Surgery in India at US$800[7]

In 2001, Dr Devi Shetty founded Narayana Hrudayalaya, a multi-specialty hospital in Bommasandra on the outskirts of Bangalore City in India. He is a man on a mission. He started this because he has a vision of providing every Indian child with good and affordable medical care.

The Indian healthcare system in India is dilapidated. Being the second most populous country in the world, the healthcare infrastructure is overburdened. Lack of healthcare insurance and a grossly inadequate public system means that 70 per cent of healthcare spending is borne by Indians out of their pocket. India requires 25 lakh (or 2.5 million) heart surgeries a year but does only 60,000. Dr Shetty believes cost of healthcare will be reduced through economies of scale. With this in mind, he pioneered the unique concept of Health City, a conglomeration of multiple super specialty hospitals in a single campus.

Today, Narayana Hrudayalaya[8] runs 5,550 beds across 14 hospitals in 11 cities. The cardiac unit in Bangalore is one of the world's largest heart hospitals performing over 30 major heart surgeries a day. The Health City also houses a centre for neurosciences, a children's hospital, a cancer research centre and a general hospital. Patients who come for treatment are not only from within India,

but also from neighbouring countries like Pakistan and Bangladesh. In the United States, open-heart surgery costs about US$100,000, depending on its complexity. At his hospitals, it costs about US$2,000 and can go as low as US$800. Patients who are better-off are charged more. For the poorest the surgery is free. How is this possible?

It starts from the planning stage. Use prefabricated building. Strip out air-conditioning, restricting it to operating wards and intensive care units. Ventilation comes from large windows in the wards. And even train visitors to help in post-operative care. Next, run the hospitals like a hybrid between Walmart and a low-cost airline. Expensive items such as heart valves are purchased in bulk like Walmart. Dr Shetty's operating theatres perform the highest number of heart surgeries daily in the world. They are run from early morning to late at night six days a week like low-cost airlines which keep their planes in the air as much as possible.

Will quality of healthcare be compromised if the focus is on driving cost down? Jack Lewin, chief executive of the American College of Cardiology, who visited Dr Shetty's facilities, says the opposite is true. Studies show quality rises at hospitals that perform more surgeries because doctors get more experience. Like Prof Philip Choo in Singapore, Dr Devi Shetty draws inspiration from the Japanese in operating the most efficient automobile assembly processes in the world. The person whom *The Wall Street Journal* calls *The Henry Ford of Heart Surgery* sums up by saying,

Japanese companies reinvented the process of making cars. That's what we are doing in healthcare. What healthcare needs is process innovation, not product innovation.

A COLLECTION OF QUESTIONS

PART 1—WHO ARE YOU?

Chapter 1: Knowing Yourself

Q1: What drives you internally? Name your top five values and rank them.

Q2: How will the people closest to you describe you, warts and all? Any surprises with reference to Q1?

Q3: What support do you need from the people closest to you to live your top values?

Chapter 2: Character Above All

Q1: Can you think of a defining moment that you have encountered? What have you learnt about your character?

Q2: You are the boss. You have a high-flying sales director who is a star in the industry. She and her team outperform year over year, resulting in strong top- and bottom-line growth for the company. She is a *prima donna* though. She rides roughshod over everybody in the company. Sparks are flying and there is static in the atmosphere. You fear that she will quit if you speak to her about her toxic behaviour. How will you handle this?

Chapter 3: The Light and the Shadow

Q1: Have you ever overused your strengths? What is the impact on yourself and others?

Q2: When was the last time you observed someone behaving out of character? Perhaps, it might have happened to you? What can you learn about this?

Q3: In your long leadership journey, how do you ensure that you are able to embrace the light and the shadow? How should you apply Derek Walcott's advice?

Q4: Dr Philip Zimbardo, professor emeritus of psychology at Stanford University, has done extensive research which shows that evil is something we are all capable of, depending on circumstances. He also asserts that we are just as capable of great heroism. What do you think? What are the circumstances that will bring out the good or evil in us?

Q5: You are about to tap a well-regarded subordinate to a high office. You have seen his light thus far. Will his shadow manifest itself when he is up there?

PART 2: THE MEANING OF YOUR WORK

Chapter 4: Serving a Larger Purpose

Q1: What is the single biggest reason you are doing what you are doing?

Q2: The strategy that the bosses (including yourself) have endorsed isn't working out. Everybody knows this. But no one wants to raise the red flag. What will you do?

Chapter 5: People Are the Best Investment

Q1: Do you believe in the saying, "People first, performance and results will follow"? How measurable is this leadership philosophy?

Q2: How do you identify the right people for your team? What difficult choices will you make to ensure you have a great team?

Q3: How do you engender a love of learning in your company?

Chapter 6: Raising Everybody's Game

Q1: Does Dr Charan's observation that "at least 50 per cent of the people in leadership positions are operating far below their assigned layer" resonate with you?

Q2: What game are you playing now? How should you raise your own game?

Q3: How regularly do you get on the balcony in the course of your work? How does it help you?

PART 3: SEEING NEW POSSIBILITIES

Chapter 7: The Whole Brian

Q1: What are you: left-brained or right-brained? How can you be whole-brained?

Q2: How will you handle the following situations?

Case 1

One of your managers, known to be a creative type, approaches you one day with an idea. She had been brainstorming with her team members. They suddenly had a flash of insight that they all feel will lead to a breakthrough in the market. The idea sounds a little wild to you. It is still in the early days. She is asking for some funding to flesh it out a little.

Case 2

During a meeting to discuss a particular project, many differing views are expressed about how to proceed. The four individuals who speak up all have valid and interesting perspectives. This much is clear. Everybody is engaged and committed to make the project a success. It is unlikely that you will be able to reach closure today on the next steps. But the deadline looms.

Case 3

You notice that over the years, your company has become dominated by the left-brained style. It has created an engineering culture that has worked very well so far. Indeed, there have been outstanding examples of creativity in innovative marketing and even clever product designs. But the environment is changing rapidly and you sense that more of the same will not cut it. You know intuitively that you will need new ideas or even new personalities to shake up the strong data-driven culture.

Chapter 8: Paradoxes

Q1: Can you think of a paradoxical situation that you have encountered? What did you feel initially? How did you finally come to terms with it?

Q2: How will you encourage people at work to view paradoxes as stimuli for creative ideas?

Q3: Do you take an active interest in philosophy, history, literature and the fine arts? What have they got to do with leadership and creativity?

Q4: Revisit Chapter 3: The Light and the Shadow. What are the common themes in Chapters 3 and 8?

Chapter 9: Deep Listening

Q1: When you speak with someone, observe how you are listening when he speaks. Observe also how he listens when you speak. What are the differences in the listening ability between the two of you?

Q2: When was the last time you listened deeply? What surprised you? How can you make deep listening a habit?

Chapter 10: Disruptive Questioning

Q1: Observe how discussions are conducted in your company. Using three to five different words, how will you describe the climate? How do participants feel as they end the meeting? Is it a problem-focused or solution-focused approach?

Q2: What steps can you take to ignite creativity in your company?

Chapter 11: Complexity

Q1: When in doubt, have you ever said, "I don't know"? When should you say this? When should you not say this?

Q2: Are you a fox or a hedgehog? In tackling complex situations, what is your preferred course of action?

Q3: We discussed the differences between technical and adaptive challenges in Chapter 6. We also mentioned the metaphors about organizations in the Introduction of this book: machine *versus* the living system. What dominant thinking influenced the CEO when he mandated the large-scale change? How will you do it now if you are in his shoes?

Q4: Observe the talented people in your organization. Do they play to win? Or do they play not to lose?

PART 4—LEADING WISELY

Chapter 12: Reflection

Q1: In the story *The Rolling Stone*, Maugham said of his subject: "The insignificance of his mien was a true index to the insignificance of his soul. Behind the blank wall was blankness." Do you agree that a person's demeanour reveals much about who he is?

Q2: How can you apply the lessons of extraordinary people as synthesized by Gardner to your own life?

Chapter 13: Self-Renewal

Q1: How can you counteract workplace stress so that you can stay healthy and calm?

Q2: We know that creativity dies under the gun. Yet, today's pressure-cooker work environment will not ameliorate. How, then, will you protect the creative side of your people?

Chapter 14: Gems in the Brain Attic

Q1: Are there gems in your brain attic? What treasures have you excavated of late? How has it happened?

Q2: What is your creative ritual?

Q3: How will you help your people become more creative?

Chapter 15: Mindfulness

Q1: If you have not done so yet, do check out the custodian-explorer continuum diagnostic in Appendix 1. What will you do to enhance your ability to lead like an explorer?

Q2: How mindful are you as a leader? What are some personal examples of mindfulness or mindlessness?

Q3: Ronnie is an archetype of a talented person consumed by his burning ambition. There are countless such people around us.

Perhaps he reminds us of someone we know? What could have saved Ronnie from himself?

Q4: In Appendix 2, we discuss healthcare services, which are heading towards crisis proportions globally. I feature two healthcare practitioners who have decided to make a difference by turning conventional medical practices on its head. Can you do the same within your own field?

Q5: As you can see, I have collated all the questions at the end of each chapter into this appendix. This serves as a refresher of topics discussed in the book. How many of these questions are pertinent to you?

ENDNOTES

INTRODUCTION

1. Two thinkers and authors have been a great source of inspiration in the preparation of this book. They are Fritjof Capra, author of *The Turning Point: Science, Society and the Rising Culture*, and Margaret J. Wheatley, author of *Leadership and the New Science: Discovering Order in a Chaotic World*. Their seminal books elucidate how the new discoveries in biology, quantum physics and chaos theory are radically altering our understanding of organizations, leadership, complexity and life. The expression *creative minorities* is from *The Turning Point*.

2. Collins, J. "How the Mighty Fall: A Primer on the Warning Signs," *Bloomberg Businessweek*, 14 May 2009.

3. Chua, A. *Day of the Empire: How Hyperpowers Rise to Global Dominance — and Why They Fail* (New York: Anchor Books, 2009).

4. Zaleznik, A. "Managers and Leaders: Are They Different?" *Harvard Business Review*, January 2004.

5. Bennis, W. *On Becoming a Leader* (New York: Addison-Wesley, 1989). In Chapter 2 of this excellent book, Bennis shares his deep insights on leadership. There is also a list of crucial differences between managers and leaders.

6. 2010 IBM Global CEO Study: Capitalizing on Complexity.

7. 2012 IBM Global CEO Study: Leading Through Connections.

8. Wheatley, M.J. *Leadership and the New Science: Discovering Order in a Chaotic World* (San Francisco, CA: Berrett-Koehler, 2006).

9. Davenport, T.H. "The Fad that Forgot People," *Fast Company*, 31 October 1995.

10. de Geus, A. *The Living Company: Habits for Survival in a Turbulent Business Environment* (Boston, MA: Harvard Business School Press, 2002).

11. Capra, F. *The Tao of Physics: An Exploration of the Parallels Between Modern Physics and Eastern Mysticism* (New York: Bantam Books, 1975).

12. An insightful discussion on Daoism can be found in Chapter 11 of the book *Indigenous and Cultural Psychology: Understanding People in Context*. The authors of the chapter are Kaiping Peng, Julie Spencer-Rodgers and Zhong Nian. The book was edited by Uichol Kim, Kuo-Shu Yang and Kwang-Kuo Hwang (New York: Springer, 2006).

13. Brooks, D. *The Social Animal: A Story of How Success Happens* (London: Short Books, 2011).

14. Wilson, T.D. *Strangers to Ourselves: Discovering the Adaptive Unconscious* (Cambridge, MA: The Belknap Press of Harvard University Press, 2002).

15. Hesse, H. *Siddhartha* (New York: Bantam Books, 1981).

Chapter 1: KNOWING YOURSELF

1. Bennis, W. *Why Leaders Can't Lead: The Unconscious Conspiracy Continues* (San Francisco, CA: Jossey-Bass, 1989).

2. George, B., et al. "Discovering Your Authentic Leadership," *Harvard Business Review*, February 2007.

3. George, B. *Authentic Leadership: Rediscovering the Secrets to Creating Lasting Value* (San Francisco, CA: Jossey-Bass, 2003).

4. O'Connor, S. "Amazon Unpacked," *Financial Times*, 8 February 2013.

5. Goleman, D. *Emotional Intelligence: Why It Matters More Than IQ* (New York: Bantam Books, 1995).

Chapter 2: CHARACTER ABOVE ALL

1. Badaracco, J.L. Jr. *Questions of Character: Illuminating the Heart of Leadership Through Literature* (Boston, MA: Harvard Business School Press, 2006).

2. Zenger, J.H. and Folkman, J.R. *The Extraordinary Leader: Turning Good Managers into Great Leaders* (New York: McGraw-Hill, 2009).

3. Badaracco, J.L. Jr. *Defining Moments: When Managers Must Choose Between Right and Right* (Boston, MA: Harvard Business School Press, 1997).

4. Does contact with the arts and humanities expand the mind and elevate the spirit? Is this the cure for the evil, bigotry and violence around us? Hitler was an ardent lover of the arts in Vienna. Mao wrote elegant poems and took great interest in calligraphy and history. Yet, both men were responsible for the greatest atrocities in the annals of mankind. For a fuller discussion, I recommend reading two articles by Diane Krieger in the Winter 2007 edition of USC Trojan Family Magazine: *Is Art Really Good for You?* and *Art for Science's Sake*.

Chapter 3: THE LIGHT AND THE SHADOW

1. London, S. "Illuminating the Shadow: An Interview with Connie Zweig," *Kindred Spirit*, Autumn 1998.

2. Stevenson, R.L. *The Strange Case of Dr Jekyll and Mr Hyde* (London: Penguin, 1886).

3. Sutton, R.I. *Good Boss, Bad Boss: How to Be the Best and Learn from the Worst* (New York: Business Plus, 2010).

4. Holland, J.G. *Life of Abraham Lincoln* (Ann Arbor: University of Michigan Library, 2005).

5. I have used the modern Pinyin system for romanization of Chinese names and terms throughout the book, except for a few spellings best known outside China in another form, such as Confucius (Kǒng Zǐ in Pinyin). Thus, instead of Taoism, Lao Tzu and *Tao Te Ching*, familiar words in the old Wade-Giles romanization system, they are shown as Daoism, Lao Zi and *Dao De Jing*, respectively, in this book.

6. You will find a number of verses from the *Dao De Jing* interspersed in various chapters of this book. These are derived from many authoritative sources including books by D.C. Lau, D.T. Suzuki, Chang Chung-Yuan, Diane Dreher, Stephen Mitchell and Thomas Cleary. The verses presented in this book are my own interpretation. Traditional

books on *The Dao* will number the verses from one to 81. I have elected to dispense with the numbering.

7. Wilhelm, R. *I Ching: Book of Changes* (Stepney, South Australia: Axiom Publishing, 2001).

8. Sweeney, S. "On the Side of Angels," *Harvard Gazette*, 10 November 2011.

9. Spreier, S.W., et al. "Leadership Run Amok: The Destructive Potential of Overachievers," *Harvard Business Review*, June 2006.

10. Kets de Vries, M.F.R. *Life and Death in the Executive Fast Lane: Essays on Irrational Organizations and Their Leaders* (San Francisco, CA: Jossey-Bass, 1995).

11. Nayar, V. "A Maverick CEO Explains How He Persuaded His Team to Leap into the Future," *Harvard Business Review*, June 2010.

12. Walcott, D. *Collected Poems 1948–1984* (London: Faber and Faber, 1986).

13. Can people learn to become good or bad regardless of their genetics, inheritance, personality or family legacy? Readers who are interested in exploring the psychology of evil are recommended to read Dr Philip Zimbardo's book *The Lucifer Effect: How Good People Turn Evil.* Do check out: http://www.ted.com/talks/philip_zimbardo_on_the_psychology_of_evil.html

Chapter 4: SERVING A LARGER PURPOSE

1. Berns, G. *Iconoclast: A Neuroscientist Reveals How to Think Differently* (Boston, MA: Harvard Business Press, 2008).

2. O'Callaghan, J. "Protest, Voter Anger Put Political Risk in Singapore's Future," *Reuters*, 15 February 2013.

3. Frankl, V. *Man's Search for Meaning* (New York: Washington Square Press, 1984).

4. Pattakos, A. *Prisoner of Our Thoughts: Victor Frankl's Principles for Discovering Meaning in Life and Work* (San Francisco, CA: Berrett-Koehler Publisher, 2004).

5. Christensen, C.M. "How Will You Measure Your Life?" *Harvard Business Review*, July–August, 2010.

Chapter 5: PEOPLE ARE THE BEST INVESTMENT

1. 2012 Towers Watson Global Workforce Study.
2. Edersheime, E.H. "Peter Drucker's 'Unfinished Chapter': The Role of the CEO," *Leader to Leader Journal*, Issue No. 45, Summer 2007.
3. Nayar, V. *Employees First, Customers Second: Turning Conventional Management Upside Down* (Boston, MA: Harvard Business School Press, 2010).
4. Hsieh, T. *Delivering Happiness: A Path to Profits, Passion and Purpose* (New York: Business Plus, 2010).
5. Nonaka, I. and Takeuchi, H. "The Wise Leader," *Harvard Business Review*, May 2011.

Chapter 6: RAISING EVERYBODY'S GAME

1. Zhuang Zi (or Chuang Zhu) was a Daoist. His namesake text is a collection of stories and monologues illustrating and expounding the teachings of the *Dao De Jing*. Both *Dao De Jing* and Zhuang Zi are the two canons that present the philosophical and practical core of classical Daoism. See Thomas Cleary's *The Essential Tao: An Initiation into the Heart of Taoism Through the Authentic Tao Te Ching and the Inner Teachings of Chuang Tzu*.
2. Charan, R., Drotter, S. and Noel, J. *The Leadership Pipeline: How to Build the Leadership-Powered Company* (San Francisco, CA: Jossey-Bass, 2001).
3. Rooke, D. and Torbert, W.R. "Seven Transformations of Leadership," *Harvard Business Review*, April 2005.
4. Heifetz, R.A. and Laurie, D.L. "The Work of Leadership," *Harvard Business Review*, January–February, 1997.
5. Tan, B.H. *The First-Time Manager in Asia: Maximizing Your Success by Blending East and West Best Practices* (Singapore: Marshall Cavendish, 2010).
6. Heifetz, R.A. and Linsky, M. *Leadership on the Line: Staying Alive Through the Dangers of Leading* (Boston, MA: Harvard Business School Press, 2006).

Chapter 7: THE WHOLE BRAIN

1. Pink, D.H. *A Whole New Brain: Why Right-Brainers Will Rule the Future* (New York: Riverhead Books, 2008).

2. Bennis, W. *On Becoming a Leader* (New York: Addison-Wesley, 1989).

3. The fable *The Heron Maiden: A Japanese Folktale* is adapted from two sources. The first is an interesting website: www.theinkbrain.wordpress. com. The second is a book by Jeannette Faurot entitled *Asian-Pacific Folktales and Legends* (New York: Touchstone, 1995).

4. Leonard, D. and Straus, S. "Putting Your Company's Whole Brain to Work," *Harvard Business Review*, July–August, 1997.

Chapter 8: PARADOXES

1. Brooks, D. *The Social Animal: A Story of How Success Happens* (London: Short Books, 2011).

2. Capra, F. *The Tao of Physics: An Exploration of the Parallels Between Modern Physics and Eastern Mysticism* (New York: Bantam Books, 1975).

3. Wheatley, M.J. *Leadership and the New Science* (San Francisco, CA: Berrett-Koehler Publishers, 1999).

4. May, M.E. *The Elegant Solution: Toyota's Formula for Mastering Innovation* (New York: Free Press, 2006). The example of Da Vinci's *Mona Lisa* as a perfect expression of paradox is found on page 146.

5. Eliot, T.S. *The Complete Poems and Plays, 1904–1950* (New York: Harcourt, Brace & World, 1971).

6. See www.chinese-poems.com/wine.html

7. Takeuchi, H., Osono, E. and Shimizu, N. "The Contradictions that Drive Toyota's Success," *Harvard Business Review*, June 2008.

8. Khanna, T., Song, J. and Lee, K. "The Paradox of Samsung's Rise," *Harvard Business Review*, July–August, 2011.

9. Wartzman, R. "Management as a Liberal Art," *Bloomberg Businessweek*, 7 August 2009.

Chapter 9: DEEP LISTENING

1. Ferrari, B.T. "The Executive's Guide to Better Listening," *McKinsey Quarterly*, February 2012.
2. Sharer, K. "Why I'm a Listener," *McKinsey Quarterly*, April 2012.
3. Covey, S.R. *The 7 Habits of Highly Effective People: Restoring the Character Ethic* (New York: Simon & Schuster, 1989).
4. There is a short story by the great Russian writer Leo Tolstoy entitled *Three Questions* that the reader will find useful. It illuminates powerfully a very human condition: we are so self-obsessed that we fail to connect with the person right in front of us. Click on www.online-literature.com/tolstoy/2736/.

Chapter 10: DISRUPTIVE QUESTIONING

1. Dyer, J.H., Gregersen, H.B. and Christensen, C.M. "The Innovator's DNA," *Harvard Business Review*, December 2009.
2. Dyer, J.H., Gregersen, H.B. and Christensen, C.M. *The Innovator's DNA: Mastering the Five Skills of Disruptive Innovators* (Boston, MA: Harvard Business School Press, 2011).
3. Radjou, N., Prabhu, J. and Ahuja, S. *Jugaad Innovation: Think Frugal, Be Flexible, Generate Breakthrough Growth* (San Francisco, CA: Jossey-Bass, 2012).
4. Krattenmaker, T. "Change Through Appreciative Inquiry," *Harvard Business Publishing Newsletters*, 1 October 2001.

Chapter 11: COMPLEXITY

1. Sargut, G. and McGrath, R.G. "Learning to Live with Complexity," *Harvard Business Review*, September 2011.
2. Horth, D.M. and Paulus, C.J. "Navigating Complex Challenges: Creative Competencies for Contemporary Leadership," *De Montfort Business Mastery Series*, 2003, 2(1):12–18.
3. Thích Nhất Hạnh is a Vietnamese Buddhist monk, teacher, author, poet and peace activist.

4. Kotter, J.P. "Accelerate," *Harvard Business Review*, November 2012.

5. Tetlock, P.E. *Expert Political Judgement: How Good Is It? How Can We Know?* (Princeton, NJ: Princeton University Press, 2005).

6. Berlin, I. *The Hedgehog and the Fox: An Essay on Tolstoy's View of History* (Chicago, IL: Ivan R. Dee, 1953).

7. Kristof, N.D. "Learning How to Think," *The New York Times*, 26 March 2009.

8. I have exercised some poetic licence in my interpretation of the wise words of Lao Zi.

9. Harford, T. *Adapt: Why Success Always Starts with Failure* (London: Abacus, 2011).

10. Lindblom, C.E. "The Science of 'Muddling Through'," *Public Administration Review*, Vol. 19, No. 2, Spring 1959; "Still Muddling, Not Yet Through," *Public Administration Review*, Vol. 39, No. 6, November–December, 1979.

11. Wheatley, M.J. and Frieze, D. "Leadership in the Age of Complexity: From Hero to Host," *Resurgence Magazine*, Winter 2011.

12. Lee, L., Horth, D.M. and Ernst, C. "Boundary Spanning in Action: Tactics for Transforming Today's Borders into Tomorrow's Frontiers," *Center for Creative Leadership, Organizational Leadership White Paper Series*, February 2012.

13. Readers who wish to understand why some talented people play not to lose rather than to win are recommended to read the excellent book explaining the differences between the growth mindset versus the fixed mindset by Professor Carol Dweck. The title of her book is *Mindset: How You Can Fulfill Your Potential* (New York: Random House, 2006).

Chapter 12: REFLECTION

1. The story *The Rolling Stone* is taken from a volume of short stories by William Somerset Maugham in his book *On a Chinese Screen*. It was published by William Heinemann Ltd in 1922. It is reprinted by permission of United Agents on behalf of The Literary Fund.

2. Gardner, H. *Extraordinary Minds: Portraits of 4 Exceptional Individuals and an Examination of Our Own Extraordinariness* (New York: Basic Books, 1997).

3. Zaltman, G. and Zaltman, L.H. *Marketing Metaphoria: What Deep Metaphors Reveal About the Minds of Consumers* (Boston, MA: Harvard Business Press, 2008).

4. Badaracco, J.L. Jr. *Defining Moments: When Managers Must Choose Between Right and Right* (Boston, MA: Harvard Business School Press, 1997).

5. Aurelius, M. *Meditations* (London: Penguin Books, 1964).

6. Bennis, W. and Thomas, R.J. "Crucibles of Leadership," *Harvard Business Review*, September 2002.

7. Nonaka, I. and Takeuchi, H. "The Wise Leader," *Harvard Business Review*, May 2011.

8. Darling, M., Parry, C. and Moore, J. "Learning in the Thick of It," *Harvard Business Review*, July–August, 2005.

Chapter 13: SELF-RENEWAL

1. Benson, H. and Procter, W. *Relaxation Revolution: Enhancing Your Personal Health Through the Science and Genetics of Mind Body Healing* (New York: Scribner, 2010).

2. Capra, F. *The Tao of Physics: An Exploration of the Parallels Between Modern Physics and Eastern Mysticism* (New York: Bantam Books, 1975).

3. Amabile, T., et al. "Creativity Under the Gun," *Harvard Business Review*, August 2002.

4. DILBERT © 1997 Scott Adams. Used by permission of UNIVERSAL UCLICK. All rights reserved.

5. Ratey, J.J. and Hagerman, E. *Spark: The Revolutionary New Science of Exercise and the Brain* (New York: Little, Brown and Company, 2008).

6. Doidge, N. *The Brain that Changes Itself: Stories of Personal Triumphs from the Frontiers of Brain Science* (London: Penguin Books, 2007).

Chapter 14: GEMS IN THE BRAIN ATTIC

1. Konnikova, M. *Master-Mind: How to Think Like Sherlock Holmes* (New York: Viking, 2013).
2. Rowan, R. *The Intuitive Manager* (Toronto, Canada: Little, Brown and Company, 1986). The expression *to peer up into the night sky and see a faint star twinkling while equally intelligent colleagues see only darkness* is from Rowan's book.
3. Benson, H. and Procter, W. *The Breakout Principle: How to Activate the Natural Trigger that Maximizes Creativity, Athletic Performance, Productivity, and Personal Well-Being* (New York: Scribner, 2003).
4. Colvin, G. *Talent Is Overrated: What Really Separates World-Class Performers from Everyone Else* (London: Nicholas Brealey Publishing, 2008).
5. Tharp, T. *The Creative Habit: Learn It and Use It for Life* (New York: Simon & Schuster, 2003).

Chapter 15: MINDFULNESS

1. Boyatzis, R. and McKee, A. *Resonant Leadership: Renewing Yourself and Connecting with Others Through Mindfulness, Hope and Compassion* (Boston, MA: Harvard Business School Press, 2005).
2. Kabat-Zinn, J. *Wherever You Go There You Are: Mindfulness Meditation in Everyday Life* (New York: Hyperion, 1994).
3. Hallowell, E.M. "Overloaded Circuits: Why Smart People Underperform," *Harvard Business Review*, January 2005.
4. Rubinstein, J.S., Meyer, D.E. and Evans, J.E. "Executive Control of Cognitive Process in Task Switching," *Journal of Experimental Psychology: Human Perception and Performance*, 2001, 27(4):763–797.
5. See the article *The Multitasking Paradox* in *Harvard Business Review*, March 2013.
6. Kabat-Zinn, J. *Coming to Our Senses: Healing Ourselves and the World Through Mindfulness* (New York: Hyperion, 2005).
7. Loori, J.D. *Riding the Ox Home: Stages on the Path of Enlightenment* (Boston, MA: Shambhala Publications, 1999).

Appendix 2: LEADING CREATIVELY IN HEALTHCARE SERVICES

1. Lim, M.K. "Singapore Health Care: A Model of Prudent, Pragmatic, Public–Private Partnership," Presentation at the International Conference on Healthcare Reforms: Asia-Pacific Experiences and Western Models, Hong Kong, in March 2011.

2. Daley, S. "Danes Rethink a Welfare State Ample to a Fault," *The New York Times*, 20 April 2013.

3. Kaplan, R.S. and Porter, M.E. "How to Solve the Cost Crisis in Health Care," *Harvard Business Review*, September 2011.

4. Loke, W.C. "Why the Future of Health Care Lies in Integration," *The Straits Times*, 8 April 2013.

5. Loke, W.C. "Winding Road Ahead for Universal Coverage," *The Straits Times*, 8 March 2013.

6. Long, S. "If It Ain't Broke, Hurry and Fix It," *The Straits Times*, 29 March 2013.

7. Plowright, A. "In India, No Frills Hospitals Offer US$800 Heart Surgery," *Agence France-Presse*, 21 April 2013.

8. Andand, G. "The Henry Ford of Heart Surgery," *The Wall Street Journal*, 25 November 2009.

INDEX